TWAYNE'S WORLD AUTHORS SERIES

A Survey of the World's Literature

Sylvia E. Bowman, Indiana University

GENERAL EDITOR

FRANCE

Maxwell A. Smith, Guerry Professor of French, Emeritus
The University of Chattanooga
Former Visiting Professor in Modern Languages
The Florida State University

EDITOR

Julian Green

(TWAS 195)

TWAYNE'S WORLD AUTHORS SERIES (TWAS)

The purpose of TWAS is to survey the major writers —novelists, dramatists, historians, poets, philosophers, and critics—of the nations of the world. Among the national literatures covered are those of Australia, Canada, China, Eastern Europe, France, Germany, Greece, India, Italy, Japan, Latin America, the Netherlands, New Zealand, Poland, Russia, Scandinavia, Spain, and the African nations, as well as Hebrew, Yiddish, and Latin Classical literatures. This survey is complemented by Twayne's United States Authors Series and English Authors Series.

The intent of each volume in these series is to present a critical-analytical study of the works of the writer; to include biographical and historical material that may be necessary for understanding, appreciation, and critical appraisal of the writer; and to present all material in clear, concise English—but not to vitiate the scholarly content of the work by doing so.

Julian Green

By GLENN S. BURNE

University of North Carolina

Twayne Publishers, Inc. :: New York

Preface

Since his first novel appeared in Paris in 1926, Julian Green has been a major French writer. He has produced an impressive body of work in several genres, and in his imaginative writings he has created a personal and unique "world" populated with powerfully drawn characters expressive of profound and universally significant human problems. For this achievement Green has received many French, English, and American literary prizes, and he was elected to the Belgian Academy. Recent studies of contemporary French writing place him in the forefront of French novelists—in the company of such notables as Gide, Camus, Mauriac, and Bernanos. There is nothing unusual about this, except the fact that Green is an American born in Paris of American parents in 1900. He is completely bilingual, and he has spent several years in America and was even a member of the United States armed forces for a time. He remains, however, little known in this country except by academics, literary critics, and other specialists on the contemporary French literary scene. This is not surprising, perhaps, because Green is thoroughly French by culture and choice of literary language: all but one of his works were written in French and published first in France. Most of his major writings have been immediately translated into English and reviewed in prominent American journals and newspapers, but this does not seem to have brought Green to the attention of the general American reader, and his works are to be found mainly in university and in larger public libraries.

This present book is intended primarily as a survey of Green's accomplishments and as an introduction to his major writings. Whereas there exist many excellent studies of Green in French, as of 1971 there is only one published full-length book in English —Samuel Stokes's *Julian Green and the Thorn of Puritanism*— and since that study was originally a doctoral dissertation examining in depth a particular aspect of Green's work, there is a place for a more general presentation which, while having some interest for the specialist, is aimed at a wider audience. For that reason the present study will include, along with critical commentary, synopses of the more representative novels and plays and will focus on major themes. I have studied Green in his original French, but for purposes of quotation, I have used translations available to the English-speaking reader—even though some of those translations, especially the earlier ones, do not render Green's prose as faithfully as one might wish. Where translations do not exist and when specific translators are not cited in the text, the translations are my own. When two publication dates are given for a specific work, the first is for the French edition; the second for the English translation.

I wish to acknowledge my debt to numerous French, English, and American critics, and especially to Green's long-time friend and fellow writer, Robert de Saint Jean, whose work *Julien Green par lui-même* makes available many revealing commentaries and explanations by Green not available anywhere else. I have also drawn extensively on Green's journals and autobiographical writings, including the one-volume edition of the journal referred to in the footnotes as JV (an abbreviation borrowed from Saint Jean). I also wish to thank Kent State University's Research Council for financial support in research and travel. And finally I wish to thank Mr. Julian Green for granting me three lengthy, enjoyable, and profitable interviews at his residence in Paris.

Kent, Ohio 1970

Acknowledgments

I should like to express my gratitude to Green's French and American publishers for permission to quote from the following works:

The Transgressor by Julian Green (*Le Malfaiteur,* copyright 1956 by Librairie Plon). Reprinted by permission of Pantheon Books of Random House, Inc.

Each in His Darkness by Julian Green (*Chaque Homme dans Sa Nuit,* copyright 1960 by Librairie Plon). Reprinted by permission of Pantheon Books of Random House, Inc.

To Leave Before Dawn by Julian Green (*Partir Avant le Jour,* copyright 1963 by Editions Bernard Grasset; copyright 1967 by Julian Green). Reprinted by permission of Harcourt Brace Jovanovich, Inc.

Permission to quote from Green's complete writings has been granted by his French publisher, Librairie Plon.

Contents

Chronology

1900	Birth, September 6, rue Ruhmkorff in Paris, of Julian Hartridge Green.
1907-1918	Study at the Lycée Janson de Sailly, Paris.
1914	December 27, death of Julian's mother.
1916	Green's renunciation of Protestantism and conversion to Catholicism.
1917	July, baccalaureate.
July, 1917-May, 1918	Service as a volunteer ambulance driver, for the American Field Service and the Red Cross, on the French and Italian fronts.
May, 1918-spring, 1919	Service in the French army.
1919	First departure for America.
1919-1921	Study at the University of Virginia. Published "The Apprentice Psychiatrist" in the *University of Virginia Magazine* (1920).
1922	July, return to France. Study of painting at the Grande-Chaumière in Paris.
1924	His first publication in France: *Pamphlet contre les Catholiques de France* under the pseudonym of Théophile Delaporte.
1926	*Mont-Cinère* (novel).
1927	*Adrienne Mesurat* (novel). Death of father. Julian goes to live with sister, Anne.
1928	*Adrienne Mesurat* receives the Prix Bookman.
1929	*Léviathan* (novel).
1930	*Le Voyageur sur la Terre* (collection of stories including "Christine," "Les Clefs de la Mort," "Léviathan," and "Le Voyageur sur la Terre."
1932	*Épaves* (novel).
1933 to Feb. 1934	Second visit to the United States.
1934	*Le Visionnaire* (novel).
1936	*Minuit* (novel).
1937	April-July, third visit to the United States.
1938	Journal I (1928-34).

1939	Summer through December, fourth visit to the United States.
1939	Journal II (1935-39). Also *Personal Record, 1928-1939*.
1940	*Varouna* (novel).
1940-1942	Residence in Baltimore, Maryland. Wrote *Memories of Happy Days* (1942).
1942	August through September, service in the American army as an instructor of French.
1943	January-December, work at the Office of War Information.
1944	Lectured and taught courses on France and French literature in various colleges throughout the United States.
1945	Returned to Paris.
1946	Journal III (1940-43).
1947	*Si j'étais vous . . .* (novel).
1949	Journal IV (1943-45).
1950	*Moira* (novel).
1951	Green receives the Grand Prix littéraire de Monaco. Publication of Journal V (1946-50). Election to the Royal Academy of Belgium.
1953	Green's debut in the theater: *Sud*.
1954	Green's second play: *L'Ennemi*.
1955	*Le Malfaiteur* (novel) and Journal VI (1950-54).
1956	Green's third play: *L'Ombre*.
1958	*Le Bel Aujourd'hui* [Journal VII (1955-58)].
1960	*Chaque Homme dans sa Nuit* (novel).
1963	*Partir avant le jour* (Autobiography I).
1964	*Mille chemins ouverts* (Autobiography II). *Diary, 1928-1957*.
1966	*Terre lointaine* (Autobiography III). Green wins the Grand Prix National des Lettres.
1967	*Vers l'invisible* (Journal VIII).
1970	Green wins the Grand Prix de L'Académie Française.
1971	*L'Autre* (Novel). Green elected to L'Académie Française.

CHAPTER 1

Julian Green: The Two Realities

I Life and Character

IN December, 1966, there appeared on the first page of the Paris newspaper, *Le Figaro Littéraire*, a large picture of Julian Green and the announcement that he had won "le grand prix national des lettres," one of France's major literary prizes. In the accompanying text Robert Kanters, a leading critic for *Le Figaro*, claimed that the choice of Green was an excellent one, because he had "added a province to literary France." He went on to say that Green, "with his language, his images, his dreams, with his interior music, has resurrected the colonial south and has achieved the ultimate triumph over the Yankees in the realms of heart and imagination." He had done this not as an American but as a man of two continents. Green was the chief passenger on the return trip of the *Mayflower* and had, in a sense, resolved the transatlantic problems posed by Henry James. He had perfectly blended the old world and the new. Irish-American by heritage and French by culture and education, Green had created a new literature devoted to the expression of the profoundest problems of the human soul and in so doing had contributed brilliantly to the grandeur of French letters. Dedicated to "la musique de la vérité," Green is "perhaps one of the last representatives of that race of writers who never for an instant renounce the nobility of their vocation."

This "grand prix" was not the first of such honors to be bestowed on the writer Green. Ever since the appearance of his first novel in 1926 he has been the recipient of prizes and critical acclaim. In France he has been for many years a major writer, which makes it the more curious that in his "own country," the United States, he remains relatively unknown.

Julian Green was born in Paris of American parents on September 6, 1900. He was educated almost entirely in French schools and in French literary culture. He has nevertheless retained his American citizenship and was in fact, for a brief time, a member of the American armed forces. His parents, both from distinguished southern families, never forgave the North for destroying southern civilization, and they filled the young Julian with tales of southern life. His father was a business man representing a southern cotton-seed oil company in Paris; his mother was a beautiful southern belle of strong religious and puritan inclinations, to whom the young Green had an extremely close attachment. Julian was the last of eight children, but he was the only son. He was raised by women and governesses, had no friends, and was a lonely child. He attended French lycées and did not learn to speak English well until he was eight or nine years old.[1] The father seems to have played a small role in the boy's life, his early years having been dominated by his mother and sisters, one of whom, Anne, was to become a successful novelist in England. Despite his lack of friends Julian seemed to be a reasonably happy child of a warm and loving family, and early critics of his writings were at a loss to explain his novels, which are some of the most anguished and tormented confessions of our time. Green's writings are works of obsession, revealing the most intimate of personal struggles with the mysteries of sex, religion, and morality, mystical experiences, and experiments with "consciousness expansion" in an effort to escape from the agonies of physical existence which, for Green, consisted of a suffocating sense of entrapment and nightmarish fatality. These works of mental torment and physical violence all derive from a man whose early life was, to all appearances, enviable in its emotional security and family serenity. But his was not an average and normal childhood, as some critics have maintained,[2] and in his recent autobiographical writings Green tells us much of the tensions and trauma that determined the obsessive character of his novels.

The outbreak of World War I had a considerable emotional impact on the Green family and probably contributed much to the death of Julian's mother (December 27, 1914), a tragedy from which it is probably accurate to say that he never really recovered. Then came the physical proximity of war itself with its growing casualty list, food rationing, and, above all, the stationing of the wounded in the Greens' apartment house. His sisters served as nurses, one of whom, Retta, died partially as a result of the exhaustion of overwork. The young Julian, then a lycée student, felt himself surrounded by suffering and death.

Green received his baccalaureate degree in July, 1917, and immediately joined the American Field Service as an ambulance driver. There he met, for the first time, American boys of his own age. He also served in the Red Cross in Italy and later as an instructor of French in the U.S. Army. But being a shy boy, he tended to keep his distance from the bumptious young Americans. He finally managed to join the French army—by the devious route of first joining the French Foreign Legion. He was discharged in 1919 as a second lieutenant and returned to Paris to pursue a career. But what career? He had decided against following his father into the business world, for which he had no taste whatsoever, and resolved to be either a painter or a writer. But first he was to come to terms with strong pressures to enter the priesthood. The discussions he had with a priest who was his spiritual director, and his own personal struggles with the problems of religious faith, are strongly reminiscent of the experiences of Joyce's Stephan Dedalus in *Portrait of the Artist as a Young Man*. In both stories the religious problems and pressures, the mental anguish leading up to the "Grand Refus," are strikingly similar. Green says:

There comes a moment in one's life when one's entire destiny is decided, but that moment is the fruit of a long series of actions which are unconsciously strung together on a secret chain. I see clearly, or think I see, the moment which decided my fate. It was, it seems to me, in April 1919, on a warm afternoon, when I was returning from a service. The ceremony had taken place in the crypt of the chapel on rue Cortambert. . . . While climbing the stairway from the crypt, I stopped for a moment on a step, my heart overflowing with sadness at the thought of the world I was going to leave behind, of all that it would be able to give me which I was rejecting in order to retire into a monastery. God only knows what took place in me at that moment. Suddenly I felt forming in me the "grand refus" which would lend such a special aspect to my life. An immense weight was lifted from me at that very instant: it was the weight of the Cross.[3]

It was shortly after this crucial experience that Green was sent, rather unwillingly, to the University of Virginia under the sponsorship of an American uncle. As a "special student" he studied languages and read widely in religion and sociology. During his first two years he remained aloof from the American students, the shy Frenchman dreaming of his native Paris. In his third year he had made a few friends and had become an assistant professor of French. He no longer felt like a foreigner, but his nostalgia remained, and in July, 1922, he returned to France, bringing with him a storehouse of memories and scenes which would figure prominently in his later writings, a rich accumulation which would be replenished on his return to America during World War II. Many of his writings—*Le Voyageur sur la terre* (*Pilgrim on the Earth*), *Moira*, *Mont-Cinère* (*Avarice House*) and *Chaque homme dans sa Nuit* (*Each in His Darkness*) along with the autobiographical *Terre Lointaine*—stem largely from his American experiences.

During his sojourn in Virginia, Green wrote his first story, his only one in English, called "The Apprentice Psychiatrist."[4] This fledgling work, although since rejected and ignored by its author as an embarrassing juvenile effort, lay the groundwork for much of Green's later writing. In its treatment of the morbid and pathological, and in its intense portrayal of introversion and insanity, brutal violence and unrelieved tragedy, it clearly foreshadows both the themes and the style of Green's mature novels. But, as a member of his family remarked: "Julian's hair stands on end at the very mention of the piece, but it is his own printed child, and I don't see very well how he can ignore it."[5] Nevertheless, unimpressed by his first publication, Green returned to France still undecided whether or not to become a writer. He tried his hand at painting, studying for a while at the Grande-Chaumière in Paris, but at that time fashions in painting were surrealistic and futuristic, and he felt strongly that he would never be a success at such modern techniques. In his bones he felt himself to be a Classicist—a feeling amply borne out by the spare style and taut construction of his fiction.

While he was in art school he fell in with a group of intellectuals, and he was asked to contribute to a new journal (*La Revue des Pamphlétaires*, October, 1924—it lasted only one issue). The result was his "Pamphlet contre les Catholiques de France" which appeared under the pseudonym of Théophile Delaporte. The piece attracted considerable attention as a result of its rather dramatic title and, as its author later confessed, "from its frenzied disregard of actuality."[6] But the pamphlet represented more than just a passing interest on Green's part. Its subject—an attack on contemporary French Catholics' flabby and halfhearted practice of their faith—formed a persistent aspect of Green's religious thinking. He was deeply read in the literature of the French and English seventeenth century and had an abiding admiration for Donne, Herbert, Vaughan, and, above all, Pascal—not just his "angoisse métaphysique" but also his hope and faith, expressed in direct, tough-minded language. The Jansenist writers of Port-Royal had also impressed him, along with the seventeenth-century Jesuit Father Seurat. Green says that what he has always liked about the writings of Port-Royal was not just their substance but their "tone"—"the way they wrote and talked about religion." Most nineteenth-century Catholic writers, on the other hand, Green always found "sickening"—especially the well-known Father Faber, whose tone is intolerably "sentimental." The writers of the earlier century were strict and forbidding, but at the same time they had an admirable feeling for religion that Green found most sympathetic.[7] And it was this contrast between the rigorous seventeenth century and the relatively flabby modern period that found its way into the young Green's pamphlet against the Catholics of contemporary France.

Meanwhile, Green had been collecting fragments and bits of unfinished stories. One of them he worked on fairly consistently, partly as experiment with character drawing, partly as a test of his own method of writing. This story began in the form of recollections drawn from his University of Virginia days but gradually lost the characteristics of autobiography. His natural bent for the supernatural took over; a plot asserted itself; and he found he had written a story, *Le Voyageur sur la Terre*. He confesses to being very uncertain about what he had created—whether it was indeed a real book or just a formless narrative: "I was at times painfully conscious that I did not write like the more successful novelists of my day, in that dazzling elliptical style, enriched with new images. What I had to say, I said in a bare, direct way, and with not the slightest desire to flatter my reader's taste. It seemed all too probable that people wouldn't care for that sort of thing."[8] As it turned out, he could not have been more wrong: it was just that bare, direct style that won the commendation of established writers like Gide and Mauriac. But, full of uncertainty about his work, Green submitted the manuscript to the judgment of a friend, the noted author Jacques Lacretelle, who approved it and sent it to Gaston Gallimard, his own publisher. Gallimard was looking for new authors at that time, and, since the publishers also owned the prestigious journal, *La Nouvelle Revue Française,* a contract with Gallimard meant possible serialization and a wide audience. A few weeks later Green signed a contract, and his career was under way under the best possible auspices.

In the same year (1925), encouraged by his friend Robert de Saint Jean (who was later to produce *Julien Green par lui-même*), Green began his first full-length novel. He spent about four months writing in the south of France, returning to Paris with the completed manuscript of *Mont-Cinère* (*Avarice House*). Saint Jean read it and, as he was a staff member of the *La Revue Hebdomadaire,* arranged for that journal to publish part of it serially. The entire novel was then taken by Plon-Nourrit, who was to be Green's principal publisher from that time on, and it appeared the following year. So the years 1925 and 1926 were of crucial importance to Green personally and professionally. His first works had been well received; success gave him confidence in himself and his mode of writing: he had found a career. He began other projects, including his second novel, *Adrienne Mesurat* (*The Closed Garden*), and a series of critical sketches to become *Suite Anglaise*: essays on Samuel Johnson, Charlotte Brontë, Charles Lamb, and William Blake. *Adrienne Mesurat* was serialized in 1926, appeared as a book in 1927, and was translated into English the next year. In America *The Closed Garden* was chosen as a Book-of-the-Month Club selection. It also won the Prix Paul Flat from the Académie Française and the Prix Femina-Bookman, which Green received in London from the hands of the novelist Hugh Walpole.

For the next ten years Green worked hard at his writing. Four novels, a collection of short stories, and two volumes of his *Journal* appeared before the war broke out in 1939. Green was in America at the time, and he returned immediately to France, where he worked for the Bureau of Propaganda in Paris. With the occupation he and his sister Anne moved south, first to Pau, then to Bordeaux. With the collapse of France he went to Lisbon and thence to the United States, where he joined American relatives in Baltimore. Though terribly upset over the fall of Fance, he did not remain idle. He accepted the hospitality of his American kin and set to work, finishing up a novel begun before the German occupation and writing volume three of his *Journal* which was understandably devoted to his reactions to the war and to his sadness over his forced exile from homeland and friends. He also wrote at this time one of his few works in English, *Memories of Happy Days* (Harpers, 1942). This book of reminiscences, written partly through the encouragement and advice of his relatives, has no French counterpart, though echoes of it are found in "Quand Nous Habitons Tous Ensemble" in *Les Oeuvres Nouvelles* (1943).

During the war years in the United States Green also kept busy with activities other than writing. Between 1940 and 1942 he gave lectures at Princeton University, a course at Goucher College, and summer lectures at Middlebury College; he was a visiting lecturer at Mills College and did radio work for various French organizations in New York City. He traveled throughout the East and saw much of other French notables exiled in America, such as the Casadesus and Maritains, and the translator Maurice Coindreau. Being an American citizen, Green was inducted into the United States Army in August, 1942, and he taught French until being discharged, shortly thereafter, as overaged. He was also associated with the French section of the Office of War Information. He returned to Paris immediately after V-J Day (September, 1945), renewing his old friendships and his life as eminent man of French letters.

One of the important developments in Green's literary career was his decision, in 1928, to keep an intimate journal. Inspired partly by the example of André Gide and partly by the needs of his own temperament, he began to keep a detailed record of his ideas, activities, conversations with friends, and, above all, reflections on personal problems which were to find their way in various forms into his novels and plays. This journal runs to several volumes, and it has done as much to establish Green's reputation in France as anything else he has done. It has provided a good portion of the interest aroused by Green, as both man and artist. On the strictly artistic level, his journals and the more recent autobiographical writings give a fascinating study of the relations between art and life, of the creative process, and the way in which lived experience becomes artistic expression. On another level, Green's confessions have provided certain critics with a field day in psychological analysis. For one of the primary elements in Green's life and work is the fact that he found himself, while still a boy, to be powerfully attracted to members of his own sex. For many years he kept his problem to himself, confiding it only to certain intimate friends and to portions of his journal he did not intend to publish. More recently, however, he has come more out into the open with what he calls his "emotional bias" and has discussed it in his autobiographical writings (*To Leave Before Dawn, Terre Lointaine*).

What complicates all this is the fact that Green is devoutly religious, having been converted in his sixteenth year from a puritanical Protestantism to an equally puritanical Catholicism. Obsessed with the idea of purity, he was horrified and confused when, during his late adolescence, he experienced a sexuality that was directed exclusively toward certain of his school fellows. For him, the flesh, the senses, became the mortal enemy, the devil incarnate, and he claims that his body became a battleground for a never-ending war between, on the one hand, Satan, the impure, and the threat of damnation literally believed in, and, on the other hand, God, purity, and salvation. The themes of religious and sexual morality are not uncommon in contemporary literature, but Green handles these problems in terms that often sound strange to modern (at least modern American) ears. His many pronouncements on sin and damnation are strongly reminiscent of early American Puritan divines, or of the French seventeenth-century Jansenists writing out of their ascetic retreats in the monastery of Port-Royal. He has been called a man of the Middle Ages, a haunted solitary obsessed by the temptations of the Devil, always seeing life as the "dance of Death"—the skull beneath the skin.

On the other hand, Green can be seen as exceedingly contemporary—in the image of "man-in-the-universe" which he projects—the lonely, alienated individual groping his way through a hostile or indifferent universe and victimized by forces which he can neither control nor understand. Green has been viewed, inevitably, as one of the first "existentialist"[10] novelists and as an originator, along with Malraux and Camus, of the "metaphysical revolt" against the human condition. For Green's characters, while they represent unique situations, also depict the universal human experience of man's confrontation with the cosmos. His antihero is a character who is acted upon rather than one who acts, who is socially inept and maladroit, gifted with a remarkable talent for mischance, and who ends up a stranger to his own life in which he participates physically but not mentally, ultimately taking defensive and usually violent action against a world in which he makes a poor showing.[11]

Green's novels demonstrate with painful vividness and intensity his conviction that the tensions of human existence, wherein man often finds himself in a state of emotional, sexual, and psychic entrapment, can find resolution only in extreme violence, in murder and rape, in futile attempts at flight, in madness and suicide. Some of his novels are Dostoevskian studies in crime and punishment, where violent transgressions against God and humanity are punished, not by organized society, but by the perpetrator himself, whose nervous system 'suffers outrageous damage as a result of his attacks on his fellow man, and who comes to recognize, as Raskolnikov did, that in murdering another being one murders oneself. But Green, unlike Dostoevsky, denies most of his heroes the possibility of enlightenment and salvation. They go down hopelessly to defeat, tormented and confused to the end, victimized by dark forces which are mysterious amalgams of inner compulsions and outer providence. For it is never clear in Green where biology leaves off and external fatality begins. Like the dramas of Eugene O'Neill, whose work is in many ways similar to Green's, tragedies are stark portrayals of internecine family warfare, mother against daughter, husband against wife, and always man against himself—to such an extent that psychological critics have accused Green of strong sadomasochistic tendencies in his choice of themes, the mutual annihilation of members of a family—especially when his own family life was supposedly so warmly affectionate.

But Green's family life had its share of covert tensions and repressed hostilities beneath its tranquil surface. In his very recent writings, Green tries to depict his family in all fairness and affection, but we see such evidences of unpleasantness, actions and statements by his mother, above all, that we scarcely

wonder that Green turned out to be sexually maladjusted, a
lonely neurotic haunted by fears, anxieties, and frustrations
which, as he himself confesses, would have driven him mad if
he had not found an outlet in his writings. As a boy he was
always kept in the most abysmal ignorance regarding the facts
of emotional and physical life, while he was encouraged in his
terrified belief in the menace of the unseen world. He was a
superstitious child, living in a home populated—largely through
the overactive imaginations of his sisters and mother—by de-
mons, ghosts, and the Devil himself (who inhabited his mother's
clothes closet, of all places). His isolation from the world about
him was enhanced by the family emphasis on the suffering and
demise of the old South—a civilization which had died a violent death. His mother "made her son and daughters the children of a country that no longer exists, but that lived in her
heart. She caused the shadow of a tragedy to hover above our
heads, saddening our brightest hours."[12] He feared that France
might also die, and this notion came back to haunt him during
the two world wars.

Green's isolation was reinforced at school, where he was
never completely accepted; even though he spoke perfect French,
he was considered a foreigner by his chauvinistic fellow students. His discovery of his "emotional bias" closed the circle of
alienation around him. He became involved in covert sexual
experiments which depressed him terribly both because he
detested his partners in these activities and because he was
sure that he had delivered himself into the hands of the devil.
He had forsaken his ideal of purity, which so dominated his
thinking, and he had embraced the impure. His recently published writings (*To Leave Before Dawn, Terre Lointaine*) have
revealed some curious circumstances contributing to the development of his overwhelming sense of sin, his hatred of the very
flesh to which he was attracted, his fear of the human body and
longing for a life free of all sexual preoccupations—circumstances which came to form the substance of his writing.

Green has given us a graphic account of some of the sources
of his sexual anguish. Peering into the semidarkness of his own
past, he says: "I see small events that have nothing to do with
the invisible world, but whose repercussion over my life has
been too powerful for me to pass them by honestly. So here

are the crude facts and their tragicomical consequences." He tells of the time when "I was innocence itself and remained so for a long time, but it is beyond doubt that, lying on my back in bed, I took pleasure in touching a body of which I was hardly conscious as forming part of myself." Suddenly his sister appeared at his bedside and yanked back the sheets, shrieked, and called his mother. Mother came, looked at him, then ran out of the room and returned almost immediately carrying a long, saw-toothed bread knife. "'I'll cut it off!' cried my mother, brandishing the bread knife. . . . In all likelihood, I would have forgotten the scene completely if I had not been reminded of it later. As to the traces it left in me, I cannot but think them to have been very deep."[13]

This experience combined in his impressionable young mind with the occasions when his mother was giving him his bath and expressed her open revulsion at the sight of his genitals, and prepared him for some devastating experiences when she took him to the art galleries. Two paintings in particular had a lasting effect: one of Gustave Doré's illustrations of Dante's *Inferno* showing a number of naked persons in Hell trying to extricate themselves from holes in the ground, and Leconte de Nouy's *The Bearers of Evil Tidings* depicting two nearly naked slaves lying at the feet of a wrathful king reclining on his divan with a bloodied sword at his side. "Seated on the floor, eyes wide with surprise and a curiosity whose nature I did not suspect, I examined the splendid, tormented bodies with which Gustave Doré peopled Dante's *Inferno*. Fear together with admiration made me so attentive that every detail found its place in my memory, adding mystery to mystery." And when his mother took him to see the Leconte de Nouy painting, "Alas, she had no idea of what she was doing, for the enemy lent me a terrible lucidity when I looked at that picture. I do not know when it first struck my eye. Probably not before I was six. After the age of eleven, I never saw it again, but between six and eleven I was often shown it, with devastating effects. I am not expressing myself too strongly. Were it not for that picture my life would not perhaps have turned out as it did." He believes that at that moment he was given "a violent and determinative shock."

In any case, there came a day when, with all the pain a man is
capable of bearing, I felt the torment of unappeased hunger. I
remember very clearly that under a kind of hallucination, I fancied
that one of the great brown bodies struck down by death [in the
Leconte de Nouy painting] really lay under my very eyes, and it
seemed as though my whole being, soul and flesh, threw itself on him.
At the same time I knew this to be an impossibility. Such painful
frustration is not to be described. It left a deep mark on me forever.
All that life could teach me about *durus amor,* I learned in the space
of a few seconds and at an age when I could not understand its
significance. All I knew was that I felt unhappy, and unhappy for
the first time in my life, without having the least idea why. It never
occurred to me that the slave in question was very closely connected
to the lost soul in *The Divine Comedy.* I only entered into such
considerations later.[14]

Shortly after viewing these pictures for the first time, the
young Julian began drawing pictures. Unconscious of doing anything wrong, he created scenes that scandalized his family.
One picture showed naked people, men and women, being
hounded and whipped by a cruel torturer. "In the perspective
given by time, I wonder if the drawing was not inspired by a
collection of Doré, but I think a strange idea lurked in my mind:
the people were being punished for being naked. Their crime
lay in not wearing clothes. . . . Fundamentally, any explanation
I gave myself about hell turned on the problem of nakedness,
with the inevitable consequence of also turning on the problem of purity."[15]

His mother also took him to the Louvre to see the sculpture
galleries. "She little knew what she was doing. She could not
suspect that I left the place in a kind of sexual intoxication that
made me suffer all the more since the precise cause of my torture was hidden from me. Nakedness, criminal nakedness, why
was it allowed to be seen: exalted, supreme, perched on pedes-
tals and seemingly trampling us underfoot?" Of his own draw-
ings of naked people he said, "what is singular about the naked
people I depicted is that none of them had a sex."[16]

Green is invariably kindly toward his mother when commenting on her unwitting role in his development of sexual neurosis.
He gives her credit for the best of intentions:

How she longed for my salvation! I did not always understand her.
She seemed to me both mysterious and wonderful. I would not like

anyone to think of her as a puritan. The very word would have horrified her, but the way she spoke to my sisters was not the way she spoke to me. I knew that she loved me with the same rather fanatical love that I myself had for her. Around her, perhaps unknowingly, she erected terrible interdicts. The idea of purity that she formed in my brain, proceeded from her misgivings. That idea has sometimes harmed me, sometimes protected me, and I am still indebted to it on many scores, for it will probably stay with me until I die. The body was the enemy, but it was also the soul's visible fortress and chiefly the temple of the Holy Ghost. Everything pertaining to the flesh became both dangerous and sacred. The flesh was to remain spotless. On that account, the least threat alarmed my mother to an unimaginable degree, the moment I was concerned. The integrity of the body was linked to the integrity of the soul. One should remain unsullied.[17]

But at the other end of the spectrum from his problems of the physical life were a series of joyful events that can only be called mystical experiences. At certain moments during his young life the dark and frightening world would become transformed, often by a visual sensation—a view of the starry heavens at night, of a lovely landscape seen through the window of a train—and suddenly he would be overwhelmed by a feeling of pure joy. He would feel himself freed from the limitations of the body and transmuted into pure spirit. Writing many years later he recalls his first "mystical experience":

In the course of these dim years, I can remember a minute of intense delight, such as I have never experienced since. Should such things be told, or should they be kept secret? There came a moment in this room when, looking up at the windowpane, I saw the dark sky and a few stars shining in it. What words can be used to express what is beyond speech? That minute was perhaps the most important one of my life and I do not know what to say about it. I was alone in the unlighted room and, my eyes raised toward the sky, I had what I can only call an outburst of love. I have loved on this earth, but never as I did during that short time, and I did not know whom I loved. Yet I knew that he was there and that, seeing me, he loved me too. How did the thought dawn on me? I do not know. I was certain that someone was there and talked to me without words. Having said this, I have said everything. Why must I write that no human speech has ever given me what I felt then for a moment just long enough to count up to ten, at a time when I was incapable of putting together a few intelligible words and did not even realize that I existed? Why must I write that I forgot that minute for years, that the stream of days and nights all but wiped it out of my consciousness? If only I had preserved it in times of trial! Why is it given back to me now? What does it all mean?[18]

So intense were these experiences and so great was the contrast between these and the opposition experience of carnal enslavement that Green became convinced of the existence of two separate realms of being, two realities: realms of body and spirit, purity and impurity, God and Devil, the absolute and the void. Thus he was able to say, in his *Journal* of 1946, that he was convinced that the "unité de personnage" that he sought would ever evade him. He was haunted by the problem which he had become accustomed to calling the problem of two realities: "the carnal reality and the metaphysical reality. Am I going to serve as their battlefield until the end of my days?" "I have tried to find an equilibrium that is increasingly menaced by the duality of my nature." For "there are two men in each of us, the one wishing always to cut the throat of the other." To a large extent, Green's novels are dramatizations, in varying forms, of this self-destructive inner conflict of divided man and are centered around two convictions: that man is on the earth to earn eternal salvation by strict adherence to the Christian life and that the conditions of human physical existence make it impossible for man to live a truly Christian life: "The union with God which is our only *raison d'être* on this planet is rendered impossible by the world and everything that gravitates around our bodies." Brooding incessantly on this dilemma, he has interwoven his writings with comments like these: "There were two kingdoms: that of God and that of the world, and these two Kingdoms expel each other from the heart of man." "What my body wants, my soul does not want." In *Chaque homme dans sa Nuit* (*Each in His Darkness*), the protagonist thinks: "There had always been a part of himself which tried to forget the other, and which it was necessary to forget if one was to live." "One could very well be two persons." "He believed, but his body did not believe." "He threw himself into that contradiction as one throws himself into a river to swim as best he can, against the current."

It is important to note, however, that in the long struggle with his *"ange noir,"* Green does not denounce the devil because of

the carnal desire he inspires, but because, to the extent that
these impulses are not reined, the devil makes man entirely
a slave to pleasure: love is placed in peril, and mortal danger
threatens the soul. "The voluptuary makes the bed for the unbeliever."[19]

The journals reiterate his desire to escape from the unceas-
ing struggle: "During my entire youth I was haunted by the
idea of an ideal world in which preoccupations of a sexual
nature do not exist." "I have always dreamed of a life where
sensuality would be absent." "To be better, to have a life beautiful and pure." "The man I would like to be will always protest against the man that I am." "There is something in pleasure
that horrifies me. . . . Since the age of twenty I have experienced
that to the point where my life seemed torn in two. I was continually in revolt against myself." "The perpetual contradiction
I see between what I do and what I believe."

But this situation is, for Green, even more complicated. While
he recognizes that the world, the flesh, and sensuality are the
implacable enemies and underminers of faith, he also recognizes, though more rarely, that faith (at least the form *his*
faith takes) has ruined the possibility of living a happy and
satisfying physical life. He says of *Moira*: "The novel I am
writing is a long cry of hatred of instinct [but] faith is the cause
of that violent conflict." He usually reserves his hatred for sex,
but occasionally he bursts out in hatred for his faith. He cannot
live with either.

So Green, whose entire work, like that of many authors, is a
lifelong effort to discover, to know, to explain himself, comes
ultimately to accept the fact that purity and perfection are impossible and indeed "inhuman," that he needs the two extremes between which he and many of his created characters
vacillate; and at times, suspended between the extremes, he experiences a lucid detachment: "Between the lapse into sin and
the repentance, there was an interval of disgust, a disgust for
the flesh and even more horrible disgust for religion." At those
times he becomes, or has the feeling of becoming, the "*grande
âme*," the man of superior soul who welcomes and needs *extremes*
in order to rise above the mediocrities of daily reality. A character in his play, *The Enemy*, says to a "mediocre" person: "You
have a small soul, a very small soul which will never go far

in either sin or in virtue." So one of the main impulses toward transcendence of daily mediocrity is faith itself: "A faith which does not provoke contradiction is a sickly and dying faith." For there is a grandeur of evil as well as of good, and in order to comprehend the grandeur of evil one must have a sense of grandeur *per se.* The point of departure, the conflict of the individual body and soul, which has already acquired cosmic dimensions in becoming a conflict between God and Devil, contains the germ of violence born of a world of extremes. But, at the same time, the initial conflict constitutes a kind of tension field engendering forces by which the author transcends the hated everyday world.[20]

Green, then, is a man who suffers acutely because of inescapable contradictions of human existence, but he also cherishes those contradictions as the source of his work as an artist and as dynamic forces providing an enlargement of vision, an expansion of consciousness, and a sense of participation in a struggle of cosmic and eternal significance. For Green is convinced that without his problems, he would not exist—at least not as an artist. Repeatedly, in his journals, he makes such comments as: "Deprive a writer of sin, and he would no longer write." "Could it be that the artist can live only in a state of sin? That the Christian life would kill him?" "A novel is made of sin [evil] as a table is made of wood." "The talent of the novelist plunges its roots deep into sin . . . the source of the novel is impure." "Must one be a believer on the one hand and a novelist on the other?" Thus we have the distinction between the Green of the *Journal,* seeking purity in order to escape a painful conflict, and the Green of the novels who needs evil in order to write. "The believer speaks in the Journal and leans looking over the shoulder of the novelist."

But to give oneself to God does not mean, if a man has been gifted as a novelist, that he must write edifying novels. No more than François Mauriac does Green seek to put his art to the service of his faith. A timorous Christian, he flatly states, will never write a good novel. He joins Mauriac in the idea that God has given to certain of his creatures a vocation of novelist and to fulfill it is the best way to please Him. In 1949 he had already observed:

Jacques Maritain has always maintained that my books are those of a man living on a mystical plane (he meant that in the largest sense) and I believe that there is indeed in my books a profound disquietude that an irreligious person might never experience. I do not try to make my books into Catholic novels. I am horrified at the thought. But I do believe that all my books, however far from ordinary and accepted religiosity they might appear to be, are no less religious in their essentials. The anguish and solitude of the characters always comes down to what I think I have called the terror of belonging to this world.

He goes on to say: "I know there is the problem of evil which one is led to describe, for what is a novel made of, if not of evil? Remove the evil and what remains? The good, that is, the white. Black is also necessary. I will be warned that I am running a risk. I will take that risk—it is part of my vocation."[21] In later life Green has admitted that he is no longer so concerned about the "risks" incurred by the total involvement in the human condition required of the novelist, just as he is not so concerned about the contradiction between religion and art expressed earlier in the *Journal*. But he reiterates that to be known as a "Catholic novelist" is a "dreadful thing" to him. He grants that Bernanos, Mauriac, and Graham Greene are successful Catholic novelists, but he cannot work in such terms: he cannot think in terms of doctrine, Church teachings, and the like.[22]

The question is largely academic, anyway, in Green's view, since a creative artist has little control over what he creates:

The true novelist does not dominate his novel; he plunges into it, he becomes his novel. Between his characters and himself, there is a complicity more profound than he even thinks, and if they sin, he also sins in some manner or other. He is everything that his book is—if he believes in it, if he lets himself go. But if he does not submit to the spell of that monstrous thing that emerges from his brain—for the novel is a monster—he will no longer write novels, he will fabricate them.

This poses a crucial problem: "I would like to know if the act of writing a novel is compatible with the state of grace. This question I neither can nor wish to answer." Many Catholic writers have faced this problem, including Mauriac who told his fellow novelists to "purify the source." To which Green replied, "I am beginning to believe there is no novel without sin

(I am not thinking of Mauriac here, but of myself), and it is a question of knowing if the novel does not require a minimum of that false freedom that sin gives, a deliverance from all constraint. Any man who trembles before sin will never write a novel."[23]

So Green is both a man of faith and a man of letters. Is there, one might ask, a common denominator in Green's personality? Apparently not. He is a man of two views, a Janus face, with the believer on one side and the novelist on the other, and they rarely communicate, if at all. A fragment from the *Journal* makes the point: "Somebody visits me and tells me that he does not understand the 'disparity' [*décalage*] that exists between my novels and the Journal! I tell him that I don't understand it more than he does, and he regards me with astonishment. But I don't know where my novels come from, what mysterious depths."[24]

It is perhaps because of this, their mysterious origins, that novels have often been called the works of the devil. Journals, however, are another matter. They are clearly the works of their author. For this reason one of the problems that troubled Green was that of the "truth" or "sincerity" of his journals, and whether they should be published at all. But the decision appears to have been made for him: in 1938 the publishers Grasset asked Green if he kept a journal, and on his saying yes, they asked to publish it. In this way the first volume, covering the period from 1928 to 1934, came to be printed. Actually Green had kept notes for ten years prior to 1928, but many of them had been thrown away or destroyed. So the "official" *Journal* begins in 1928.[25]

Two main currents run throughout the *Journal*: the fascination for the absolute, and the search, without regard for consequences, for the truth. There are no concessions to convention or prejudice, though Green is careful not to implicate living relatives or friends. Whether the issue is religion or sex, the goal is the same—to get the right facts, the right tone. However, says Green, "in general, one does not tell all—one tries to achieve a kind of unity of being [*unité de personnage*], but on what level will that unity be achieved? On the carnal or the spiritual? Whichever the author might choose, he will cheat. He might indeed speak the truth of the soul, but not that of the body."

Green insists on making this point: that his diary offers only a fragmentary and hence partial, even falsified view. Neither his most excruciating struggles nor his most ecstatic moments are recorded there—those moments during which physical delight transcends the body and becomes a means of knowledge. He tells his readers that the highest and lowest in his life are omitted. He does not try to reconcile his contradictions—a self-imposed rule—nor to repudiate the "successive selves which had been his life before reaching the present, and equally transient ego." For "solidarity with our past is solidarity with death. I have varied. I still shall vary. . . . Baudelaire lamented that among the Rights of Man, the right of contradicting oneself should have been omitted."

But to put exclusive stress on Green's inner drama of flesh versus spirit is to give an unnecessarily severe picture of the *Journal*. It also abounds in fascinating descriptions of people and places, and offers interesting commentaries on other writers, on works of art, countrysides, and music—especially music. And he includes many charming recollections of childhood—that period of life so crucial to all men, and especially to the artist: "the child dictates and the man writes. Why, then, is it so difficult for me to reproduce in a book the true language of childhood?" Childhood resists the passage of years. It is "the limpid source in the depths of one's being that nourishes the soul, the subterranean stream that runs obscurely through adult life." "Childhood is always with us." Green was always a perceptive self-critic, and a remarkably honest one, and he is probably aware of what he reveals about his relations with the people he most loved and whose memories he most cherished.

One mental hazard that confronts novelists who keep journals did not trouble Green: he was convinced that he did not drain off his creative power in taking his daily notes and keeping a journal. To the contrary. But he was haunted by his failure to emerge from his solitude and to communicate with others. This he would only do in his plays and novels. "My true journal is in my novels." "I have almost never had the desire to write about what I had most at heart, unless it might be transposed in a novel." He says of his play *Sud*: "This play is the fruit of the experience of a great part of my life and I have put myself completely into it, but that is true of everything I write." But he adds: "Sincerity is a gift like any other gift. He is not sincere who just wants to be."

There is more biography, more tapping of the rich years of childhood, in the novels than in the journals: "Perhaps my novels and the two plays I have written explain myself better than this journal where I nevertheless try to say everything." "I would like to tell the truth about myself. . . . I would like to tell MY truth some day, some hour, or only for a few minutes. . . . I do not see any other way of drawing myself out except by writing a novel."

II *Vision into Art: The Major Themes*

It is apparent that the most valid generalization that can be made about Julian Green is that everything in his life and work is characterized by a dualism: he is a man divided against himself in almost every respect, but we are not surprised to find that his writing falls, broadly speaking, into two classes, and almost seems to be the work of two authors. One of these authors is a scrupulous realist in the tradition of Balzac and Flaubert; the other is a fantasist and melodramatist out of the era of Hoffmann and Poe. But both authors converge in some of the novels to show us that Green is, above all—a *visionary,* a man who sees beyond the agonies of his world and who devises means of escape into the realms of fantasy and dream. This phenomenon is perhaps best exemplified in an early work entitled *Le Visionnaire* (translated as *The Dreamer,* 1934). This novel depicts the fantasy life of a young man, Manuel, who finds his everyday real life to be insupportable. He is tormented by desires, frustrations, and conflicts which he cannot resolve, and so he indulges in fantasies which become increasingly vivid and real to him, ultimately supplanting his "real" life entirely. As is frequent in Green's writings, the reader is given a double point of view. At times we live through young Manuel's fantasy life, and at other times we see him through the eyes of another narrator in the tale, a girl cousin with whom he is in love. But for a long time in the story we are unsure which version, Manuel's or the girl's, is the correct one, and while Manuel's vision is dispelled at the end, we are still uncertain which reality is the most real.

This is characteristic of Green's work—the interpenetration of two worlds, the dissolving of one reality into another, the uncertainty of whether one is dreaming or awake, and the suggestion that it does not much matter, since dreams are as real as whatever our waking lives consist of. Green, in his *Journal*, quotes Gide as saying to him that what is true in his (Green's) novels is true in spite of an evident disaccord with everyday reality. This ambivalent quality is found in Green's earliest work, in stories he wrote while trying to find himself as a novelist. One of his first short novels, *Pilgrim on the Earth*, began in the form of recollections drawn from his stay at the University of Virginia, but gradually lost the characteristics of autobiography. The supernatural began to take over the narrative and became partly psychological and partly supernatural—like a fantastic tale out of Gothic Romanticism.

This preoccupation with the unseen world and with the power of the imagination to achieve a second and higher reality is characteristic of some of his early stories, of his later play *L'Ennemi* (1954), and also of the middle period of Green's career when, temporarily at odds with the Catholic Church, he was immersed in the studies of Oriental religion. During this period, the 1930's and 1940's, he wrote three novels—*Minuit* (*Midnight*), *Varouna* (*Then Shall the Dust Return*), and *Si j'étais vous* (*If I Were You*)—all concerned with the possibility of man's escaping from the limitations of the physical self, imprisoned by time and space, and finding a new identity and a new form of existence. *Midnight* (1936) is the story of a girl who flees from ordinary life with friends and family, only to become a prisoner of a distant relative who keeps a bizarre group of persons captive in an ancient mansion, gathering them around him at midnight to teach them the superiority of nocturnal existence and the power of the individual mind, at night, to create a fantasmal world infinitely better than the world of commonplace daylight. In *If I Were You* (1947, 1949) a young man is granted a wish—the power to trade places with anyone he chooses, to enter into that person's body and mind, trading lives with him, while retaining enough awareness of his original identity to enable him to regain, at the end, his first body.

Varouna (*Then Shall the Dust Return,* 1940, 1941) is the story
of two people living through a series of reincarnations, having
their love frustrated during their early lives, and, on one occasion, even killing each other, and finally achieving unity in
their last incarnation. It is a strange story, suggesting that the
individual soul is not bounded by time and space and that
it might require a succession of lives for individual destinies to
be realized.

Now the reader is entitled to ask, does Green believe, in
any sense of the word, in these ideas? This is an unanswer-
able question, because Green is dealing with realms of possibility which are ultimately unknowable, and the lines between
literal reality, fantasy, and pure hallucination are never clearly
drawn. The author, one feels sure, is as uncertain about the
reality of these stories as his readers are.

Interesting as these middle-period stories might be, many
critics do not consider them to be "true Green." His first four
full-length novels, and his last two, are probably his best. They
can be described as psychological studies with metaphysical
implications. They focus sharply on a single individual and
follow step by step the struggles of that individual to escape
his destiny—the passions, fears, and obsessions which ultimately
overwhelm and destroy him along with those persons who are
involved with him. For individual destinies are shown to be
fatally interlocked, and the strugglings in one part of the web
radiate out to affect all the others.

The first two novels, written when Green was in his mid-
twenties, are *Mont-Cinère* (*Avarice House,* 1926, 1927) and
Adrienne Mesurat (*The Closed Garden,* 1927, 1928). They are
similar in character and theme. Each novel presents a situation
typical of Green's early work: a young person, in this case a
girl, living in a gloomy provincial house dominated by a single
parent (the other is always missing), a parent who is tyrannical
and oppressive. Each novel is centered around a single theme,
and each character is the victim of a single dominant passion.
With Adrienne of *The Closed Garden* it is the compulsion to
escape the home which is a prison, and with Emily of *Avarice
House* it is the obsessive desire to possess the family mansion
and all that it contains. One novel is set in the American South
and the other in provincial France, but it does not much matter

as both are realms of Green's creation, wherein scenes and objects are described and dwelt on with such intensity that they gradually become hallucinatory, almost surreal. Like Graham Greene, Julian Green has invented his own "Greenland." His atmosphere is one of dream, or rather nightmare. That is, objects and actions are seen with the unnatural vividness characteristic of dreams, and people move, or are driven to move, in strange ways suggesting the puppet manner of dream figures, while nevertheless remaining real people. The presentation is both naturalistic and phantasmagoric, a style that one French critic has aptly called *"le réalisme magique."*

Both stories end tragically. Adrienne is driven to kill her father by pushing him down a dark staircase (whether intentionally or inadvertently is never determined, and she is never charged).[26] She then tries repeatedly to leave the empty house, but all of her brief ventures into the outside world are abortive, and she is compelled to return to her hated home, a victim of terrors (real or imaginary) and of her own ingrained habits which she cannot break. She gradually goes mad, and in the end we see her wandering the streets around her house still thinking she is making a kind of escape. It is a forceful and convincing portrait of the conditions making for insanity and of the gradual collapse of a tortured mind. In this connection, it is interesting to note that Green had never studied psychology. If he had, he says, he probably would not have written the books he did or the way he did. But he admits to being pleased that the psychologist Wilhelm Stekel said of *Adrienne Mesurat* that it was a novel of a psychological nature written by someone who obviously had no formal knowledge of psychoanalysis but who had intuitively arrived at a vivid depiction of the workings of the human mind.[27]

Emily of *Avarice House* also ends up mad. As the translated title suggests, the main characters of the study are embodiments of the single passion of avarice. The mother, a fanatical miser, tries to sell the family belongings for hard cash, whereas the daughter, aware that the old mansion and all it contains will someday be hers, fights to keep everything intact, but she ultimately succeeds only in destroying by fire the mansion and all that it contains, including herself.

Having created and established his Greenian world in his

first two novels—a world in which external conditions combine
with internal weaknesses of character to demolish the mental
equilibrium of the isolated individual—Green then turns, in his
third novel, to the theme introduced earlier in this discussion,
the theme which will dominate most of his later work: sexual
obsession, characterized by the ceaseless struggle in the soul of
man between the yearning for purity and the Christian life
and the invincible demands of the flesh. The third novel,
Léviathan (*The Dark Journey,* 1929), is a crime-and-punishment
story of a man, inept and ill-favored, who is driven by lust, frustration, and jealousy to attack the young woman he has so futilely
loved. He disfigures her horribly, and thinking he has killed her,
he flees into the night, striking down an old man who happens
to get in his way, then returns later to lurk about in the town
like the ghost of his own crime. He is ultimately revealed to
the police by a neurotic woman who has gained gratification by
her capacity to identify with the murderer's crimes. This novel
has more variety in it than the other novels, more characters,
each animated by a dominate motivation: the murderer Guéret
by desire; his beloved Angèle by the instinct of self-preservation;
Madame Londe, proprietress of the local café, by love of power
supported by curiosity—the desire to know of the intimate affairs
of her clients; Madame Grosgeorges, wife of a self-satisfied
solid citizen, by boredom. In each case, passion works to the
destruction of the individual.

In the working out of these motives and the intertanglings
of the various lives we see the unexpected, the incalculable, and
the incongruous in human affairs. This unexpectedness, with the
recurrent references to fate, gives to the story its interest, its
uncanny power. The careful realism of the provincial background, the discreetly caricatured portraits of the bourgeoisie
at Mme Londe's table, recall the art of Flaubert and Maupas-
sant, whereas the psychological study of the murderer Guéret—
his crime, his flight, and his hovering return—is strongly reminiscent of Dostoevsky. There is much use of symbolic imagery
—walls, rooms and windows, and the dark staircase which figure
significantly in the early two novels—and there are some brilliantly rendered scenes: Guéret's desperate attempts to scale a
high wall and to gain entrance to Angèle's room, and the moon-
light scene in the coalyard where the murderer has taken refuge.

This thematic use of symbolic imagery is continued in the dark nocturnal streets, the womblike and prisonlike rooms, the ever-present mirrors, and the mysterious on-flowing river of *Épaves* (*The Strange River*, 1932). This novel is primarily a psychological study of the effects of idleness and extreme self-absorption on a wealthy bourgeois who is in almost every respect the opposite of the wretched Guéret. Philip knows nothing of passion; he is in love with no one but himself; and because of his vanity and cowardice, he is totally incapable of physical action. His only real emotions are fear and guilt, and his only positive "act" is to arrive at a limited understanding and acceptance of himself. This theme of guilt, of the haunting presence of a shameful past, will also be portrayed in one of Green's three plays, *L'Ombre* (1956), with the added element of atonement through suicide. The decision to join his wife in death—a wife he had caused to be murdered—is the only "solution" available to the Philip of the play, but it is quite beyond the Philip of the novel, who meditates on suicide but is hopelessly incapable of working up the intensity of emotion necessary for the act itself.

Another of Green's major themes, one which figures prominently in his autobiographical writings, is given explicit treatment in the early *L'Autre Sommeil* and in two of his later works. The problem of homosexual love had been, in Green's view, grossly exploited and distorted by many modern writers, and in his novel *Le Malfaiteur* (*The Transgressor*, 1955, 1957) and his play *Sud* (*South*, 1953), he tries to dramatize "impossible love" as it really is—in all its spiritual and emotional as well as physical intensity. He shows us the inevitably tragic results of a love that is authentic and valid in its own terms but "impossible" in our modern cultural setting, where it is misunderstood or not even recognized—and, if recognized, pronounced shameful and driven underground. Denied the opportunity for honest expression, the victims of homosexual love are impelled to violence—but a violence directed at themselves alone, with the supreme irony being that "normal society" usually remains ignorant to the end of the homosexual's emotions or even of the fact that he has arranged his own extinction. In another time or place, the point is made, such love would have its rightful role, but here and now—impossible.

Homosexual love also figures in Green's last two novels
(to date: 1970), *Moira* (1950, 1951) and *Chaque homme dans
sa Nuit* (*Each in His Darkness*, 1960, 1961), but in minor roles.
In these works Green turns to the scenes of his first stories, the
southeastern United States of his youthful years, and in returning to those years, he also returns to what is in fact his only
subject: himself when young. Indeed he has often stated that
childhood, youth, and young manhood are the only periods of
interest for him—the years of maturity he will leave for other
authors to explore. In each of these works, then, Green has
projected part of his essential young self—in the portrait of
Joseph Day of *Moira*, a fanatical religious puritan obsessed by
his archenemy, sex, and in Wilfred Ingram (*Each in His Darkness*), a wanton young debauchee haunted by religious remorse
and desire for purity. For Green admits to a great respect and
fascination for the two inhabitants of the "Absolute": the saint
and the debauchee. In *Moira* the young Joseph tries to live the
life of a saint in a corrupt world and fails; in *Each in His Darkness* Wilfred tries to live a life of unreflective licentiousness, beyond the claims of religious faith, and fails. Each character
represents an extreme case, a form of absolutist; between them
they portray vividly the essential contradictions, the unresolv-
able conflicts, that constitute life in this world—at least for the
man who conceives of himself as both a physical and spiritual
being.

CHAPTER 2

Strangers on the Earth:
The Early Short Fiction

DURING his late twenties Green wrote several brief works
—short stories and novellas—which were immediately published and well received. The early short writings, far too ac-
complished to be called mere "apprentice works," established
for the young author both his subjects and his style. The characters and their special problems and the settings, the tone, and
atmosphere created in these stories remain unchanged in their
essentials throughout Green's long writing career. The pattern
is as follows: he begins with a lonely child living with a single
parent (the other is usually missing); other members of the
family are living in the same house but the child will have no
meaningful relationship with them. Lacking normal love and
attention and usually having no friends his own age, he (or
she) turns inward and creates his own world derived from a
lively imagination and a strong sense of the presence of a spirit
realm, a mystical "beyond." He is subject to visions and dreams
which become more real to him than "reality" itself. He ultimately rebels against his environment or tries to escape from
it, often under the influence of "another"—a second self that
speaks to him and directs him. As he grows older he will usually
commit acts of violence and suffer from mental derangement, as
he finds he cannot escape what appears to be his special destiny.

The settings tend to be old, gloomy houses, with empty rooms
and few inhabitants. The protagonists' rooms, where most of
Green's plots take place, may be places of refuge but are more
apt to become cells of a prison. The oppressive atmosphere is
enhanced by certain objects: statues and mannequins which
assume lives of their own, mottos over doorways and pictures
on walls; and sounds: echoes, creaking stairways, muffled voices.
The houses and rooms are distinct "presences" and exert a marked

influence on their inmates. Domestic existence within their
dreary walls is one of habit and routine, an insulation from the
outer world which is broken by some kind of intrusion, the
arrival of a "stranger" from the outside world who shatters the
routine and brings chaos to the orderly but deadly life within
the household or within the cloistered life of the individual:
Jalon in *The Keys of Death,* the girl Christine in the story by
the same name, Max in *Each in His Darkness,* Gaston in *The
Transgressor,* the murdered woman in *The Strange River,* the
stranger Paul in *Pilgrim on the Earth.* Whether the intrusion is
literally the moving of a newcomer into a family household or
is a breaking of some outside "force" through the insulating
shell of routine with which an individual character protects himself from the world, the results are inevitably disastrous. People
are forced to confront challenges, to face up to their own unsuspected selves, to take actions they are incapable of carrying
out, to overcome forces whose existences they had never before
suspected, and they all fail. The respectable bourgeois houses,
which are but counterparts of their respectable bourgeois occu-
pants, are brought to ruin: the fire that destroys the old mansion
in *Avarice House* has its parallel in the fires of passion and violence that consume the characters.

The early stories, like the later novels and journals, have a
great verbal simplicity and directness of style, along with com-
plexity and occasional obscurity of substance. The stories begin
and end with mystery, the mysterious unknown which is life
itself. However, elements of fantasy, dream, and symbolism
of the early stories encourage allegorical interpretations which
the later novels do not invite. The ambivalence and ambiguity of
these early stories, embodying experiences which lie largely
beyond the rational and intelligible, are provocative and suggest interpretations, but they deny full comprehension.

Most of the action in Green's stories takes place in enclosed
places, behind walls and in small rooms. But in his occasional
depiction of landscapes he always shows decided preferences:
he associates peace and sanctuary with woods and forest lands;
he abhors the sea and has small liking for mountains. He feels
at ease only in the great green forests of the north, but when
these are not available, any nearby grove of trees will do to

provide a sense of solace and peace. Green's conception of the forest is not the fearful and dark *"selva oscura"* of Dante and the Gothic romances, but more the mythic "sacred wood" in which marvelous things take place. To the young John in *The Keys of Death* a single leafy tree suffices to hide him. Its heavy branches, reaching the ground on all sides, imprison the boy in a miraculous darkness where he can see without being seen, where he feels invulnerable. In *The Dreamer* both Manuel and the vicomtesse experience the forest park around the castle as a sanctuary from death. "For as long as I can remember," says Green, "I have loved the presence of trees and the sound of wind in the leaves. . . . In the peace of these woods, I am reminded of the words of Saint Bernard: 'You will find in the woods something more than in books.' "[1] As the critic Saint Jean has expressed it, in the solitude and silence of arboreal retreats Green's "inner voice" can be heard more distinctly than in the town.

The sea, on the other hand, the few times it appears in his writings, is associated with nameless fear of the void and source of destructive elements for man. It is in this guise that the sea appears in the early story, "Léviathan," a name which Green also gave to a later novel where man's fate is associated with obscure forces which, like fabled monsters of the deep, lie beneath the surface of life.

I   *"Léviathan"*

"Léviathan" (1927) is the story of a strange, solitary man who is the only passenger on a freighter traveling from France to America. He speaks to no one and keeps to his room as much as possible—which he has arranged to look like his permanent home. He has put his books on shelves intended to hold shoes. His own blanket is thrown over the bed to hide the ship's company monogram. He has removed other evidences of the monogram and has rearranged the cabin's few furnishings. During the long passage (twenty days) the captain, a self-assured, outspoken man of modest intelligence, insists on the passenger's dining with him each day—this despite the passenger's obvious distaste for company. The traveler refuses to utter a word for almost the entire trip. At first the captain is irritated by the passenger's unresponsiveness; then he is piqued by curiosity and enjoys the "game" of trying to draw the fellow out; and finally he loses interest and lapses into indifference, though aware that all is not well with his passenger.

The story stresses the solitude of sea travel, the need to seek human companionship and conversation, even with disagreeable people. One has the sense of the voyage continuing indefinitely, with the monotony tempered by the sinister awareness of the vast and mysterious sea surrounding one—the "leviathan" ever lying in wait outside, driving even unsociable persons to seek out their fellows. The passenger is afraid of the sea, which he gazes at "with the horrified expression of a man brought suddenly face to face with death."

The last day before reaching land, the passenger breaks his silence with a confession: he has committed a terrible crime that requires him to leave France—he is, as he says, "uneasy in his mind." The captain is unimpressed. He says it is not much of a crime and that there must be more to it. (The exact nature of the passenger's confession is not revealed to the reader.) Whereupon the passenger vehemently denies all that he has just said, pounds the table, and declares that he is merely going to America on business and that it was "not a murder at all." (The captain was evidently thinking of a lesser crime.) At that, the captain smiles and insists that the man *is* a murderer, but that he (the passenger) has nothing to fear from him. Land is sighted, the captain leaves, and minutes later the passenger is carried from the ship, dead.

The story has some typical Greenian elements. It is a personal projection of Green's fear of the sea and his hatred of sea-travel, but the central metaphor is that of the confrontation of the solitary, reclusive stranger, the "outsider," with the bluff, confident, well-adjusted man of the world, the world in this instance being the ship. But, in common with Green's other short works, this story is more obscure, more symbolic than the novels. It invites allegorical interpretation: the lonely crossing in the ship of life, threatened obscurely by the pervasive elements—ennui and death—supervised by the solid bourgeois who is emphatically in charge. (The captain says, "On board this ship what I want is always necessary.") The traveler must prove his identity (passport) and submit, however unwillingly, to the customs of life at sea (face the captain at meals), but he resists change, minimizing the voyage aspect by arranging a most transitory situation, his cabin, to look like a permanent home.

The confession of guilt for crime is important only to the confessor, not to the representative of society—a crime that was probably the product of imagination (except that, in the Kafka-like sense that pervades Green's work, we are all criminals, all guilty). The traveler dies, his fate coming from within, death intervening just before he reaches his ostensible goal, America, which was not really his goal at all. His goal was death.

The passenger remains nameless, but the ship has a name: *Bonne Espérance*. But whatever man may hope for, his destiny is fixed. The story suggests that the "leviathan" is individual fatality: the *"condition humaine"* to be explored and elaborated in all the later works and given special stress in the novel *Léviathan (The Dark Journey)* in which the most recurrent term is the word "fate."

II *"Christine"*

The short story "Christine"[2] also presents a situation that is typically Greenian: the story centers around a child with only one parent, the other unaccountably missing, a child without friends. It is an adult world in a typical setting—a large, lonely house exuding an air of mystery and solitude. It is "an old puritan house" with religious mottos lettered over doorways: "In God We Trust" set in Rhode Island flint, "the hardest material in the world," along with various excerpts from the Psalms. The large, empty rooms, when disturbed, give off hollow sounds suggesting echoes: "You had the impression that someone beside you was repeating the last part of your sentence." One spoke less often and more quietly than is customary. (A good example of Green's way of creating atmosphere and portentiousness by use of concrete imagery.) The narrator, John, is a boy of thirteen. Through his eyes we see his grim and gloomy maiden Aunt Judith, who comes to visit, bringing with her a beautiful young girl, Christine. We see the girl only once, observe that she seems to carry a fixed stare on her blank, pretty face. She is confined to an upstairs room, and we do not see her again, except partly and indirectly when John peers at her through the keyhole. For John is forbidden to see the girl or to try to speak to her. Under pressure of this interdict, John becomes transformed; he broods somberly on a fixed idea, becoming obsessed by the desire to see Christine again. To ensure the boy's obedience, the aunt tells him a tale about a sinister "presence" that exists on the second floor, a thing whose warm breath can be felt when it passes in the hallway. The boy is terrified and resolves to stay off the stairs after dark. Furthermore, he is made to swear on the Bible that he will not go near the girl's room while his mother and aunt go into the town for a doctor. (The girl had had hysterics during a thunderstorm.) But the promise is soon broken under pressure of his obsession. He braves the stairway and hall. Peering through the keyhole, he is astonished to see the girl's face, lit up by a wild but blank beauty, staring curiously and uncomprehendingly at the doorway. The boy takes a ring from his aunt's trunk and slides it under the door as a gift for Christine. When, a little later, Christine departs with the aunt, the ring is stuck on her thumb. About a year and a half later, just before Christmas, the aunt visits again, this time alone. She sobbingly tells of Christine's death. The ring is now on the aunt's finger.

This story, one of Green's most provocative, works largely through allusion, symbol, and suggestion. The story functions on two levels: the psychological and the religious. On the psychological (and realistic) level, we find that the aunt had never married, and we do not know why. Christine appears to be the illegitimate daughter of the aunt—John notices in passing that there are certain facial resemblances. On this level, the story implies a sexual significance; but this is overshadowed by, or rather subsumed under, the religious implication. It is apparent that Christine is totally mad and must be kept in seclusion. The great, empty house, full of echoes, is marked up with religious mottos but devoid of real religious experience or feeling. Then enters Christine, whose name suggests Christianity, as a vision of incredible yet unattainable beauty, bringing to John both pleasure and pain, hope and despair. When she is secluded from the sight and reach of the transfigured boy, his normal obedience is quickly undermined by overwhelming desire: the quest for supernal beauty (Christianity) renders ordinary mundane strictures irrelevant. Threats of a superstitious nature do not keep the boy from attempting to gain access to the object of desire. A written message is meaningless since beauty is irrational, beyond intellect, a mindless being-in-itself. The gift of the sapphire ring, a gift to newly discovered beauty, is also a gesture of marriage (which may account for the unmarried aunt transferring the ring to her own hand). The mother and aunt say nothing of John's transgression: they perhaps sense that it lay outside and beyond their trivial efforts at familial control. Perhaps they also sense the homage due and paid to the beautiful and mad little girl. The aunt's final visit and revelation of the girl's death is accompanied by "mournful thuds" of sand being shoveled outside the window, as in counterpoint to John's awareness that the beauty, which had briefly entered his young world and transfigured it, had passed out of it irrevocably.

III   Pilgrim on the Earth

One of Green's first novellas, *Voyageur sur la Terre* (*Pilgrim on the Earth*) was published in 1926[3] and grew out of his experiences in the American south a few years earlier. During his sojourn at the University of Virginia, the young Green kept aloof from the other students and suffered from homesickness and boredom. He spent most of his time reading, omnivorously he says, in the university library, and he wrote his first story at that time, "The Apprentice Psychiatrist."[4] He spent an August vacation at his uncle's home in Virginia, a "gaunt old place," and was struck at the time by the idea that it would make an admirable setting for a story.[5] These visual experiences combined with remembered emotional experiences a few years later to produce *Voyageur,* a very personal narrativè involving Green's struggles with the problem of purity and impurity and centering around the idea of the "double." As with most of Green's writing, the narrative was composed virtually unconsciously; he was totally involved in the story during its composition and had no sense of its import or direction as he proceeded. He says, "I was unaware for a long time, while I was writing the story, that Paul was the double of Daniel O'Donovan."[6] And as one critic says of this work: "The reader will understand a certain page, a certain chapter, often *better and sooner than the author* [his italics], a phenomenon that is very possible in England and the

United States, and also in Russia (Dostoevsky and his public), but rather rare in France where the writer . . . is even more cunning than Monsieur Everyman, which is saying a lot."[7] Green has said much the same thing about his other works: that he has no idea where he is going when he is in the throes of composition.

The story is worth discussing in some detail, because, written when the author was only twenty-six, it contains in embryo the themes which dominate Green's writings for the rest of his career: the ceaseless struggle, within the soul of a lonely individual, between the contrary demands of the flesh and the spiritual life, between purity and impurity; the intertwining of reality and dream, reality and hallucination, the interpenetration of the visible and invisible worlds; the conviction that each man is in fact two persons, or that one is frequently "possessed" by some stronger will, some outside being who enters and controls one and who speaks in a strange but somehow familiar voice, urging action or counseling restraint. The idea of the double or alter ego is, of course, not peculiar to Green. He began writing at a time when the idea figured prominently in the work of major writers, and had for nearly a hundred years. Green, very much aware of the stories of Poe, had doubtless read "William Wilson," first published in 1839; Dostoevsky (whom Green says he did not read until he was nearly fifty) built many of his characterizations around the idea, and not just in his short novel, *The Double*. There followed Wilde's *Picture of Dorian Gray*, Yeats's "antithetical man," Stevenson's Jekyll and Hyde, and Conrad's many secret sharers. So Green was working in a well-established tradition. But readers of his journals and autobiographies are aware that Green did not need a tradition or models: his personal experiences, his own haunted life, gave him ample evidence to support the idea that man's range of existence is not bounded by one body limited to one time and one place, and the mysterious identity of Daniel O'Donovan and his "friend" Paul is but the first in a long series of divided personalities. The only question, one that cannot be answered, is whether Green's cases of "*dédoublement*" are to be seen as having some form of "real" existence or are merely products of the characters' mental derangement. Some works, such as *Pilgrim on the Earth*, appear to stress the latter view; others stress the former. But they are always highly ambiguous. They are presented as intensely felt experiences, and we are left to make our own judgments. In this respect, Green's style deserves comment. In this first short novel, he establishes a mode of expression which changes very little as he develops his art: a simplicity and directness of language, a spareness that can hardly be called "style" at all. It stems from the immediate involvement of the author in his work: he cannot "distance" his writing by anything like a style, and we, as readers, are similarly involved. Green's is an unobtrusive prose that "takes us in" and suspends critical faculties until the story is ended and we can reflect on our imaginative experiences while reading.

This story, like another short work, *Les Clefs de la Mort* (*The Keys of Death*), begins with a familiar romantic device: a strange occurrence, the unaccountable death of a young man, which creates a mystery which can only be solved, if at all, by seeking evidence in old but recently discovered manuscripts and letters which offer more mystification than light and leave things pretty much as they were—a mystery. This story begins, then, with the narrator puzzling over the death of Daniel O'Donovan. The causes of his fall into a rocky ravine are so obscure that, despairing of determining foul play, accident, or suicide, persons aware of the event have decided that it was death "by the visitation of God." The inscription on the victim's tombstone— "How shall a young man cleanse his way?"—is of little help: but it does serve to give a religious aspect to the story and suggest the importance of Green's concern for the problem of purity.

After a brief introduction by the unnamed first narrator, the story shifts to the discovered manuscript written by a certain Daniel O'Donovan, and we learn some important things about Daniel's boyhood. He had been an orphan living in a large, gloomy house with his uncle, aunt, and the uncle's frightening father-in-law. Daniel, like all of Green's young protagonists, is lonely and withdrawn, and has no meaningful relationship with his relatives. He spends much time in his room, which is decorated with religious mottos—at the instigation of his aunt, a superstitious old puritan from Providence. The motto says something about someone always being in the room with you and listening to what you say. The boy's window provides a view of a nearby church, and Daniel lives in fear that the church will catch fire and collapse on his part of the house. The other inmates of the old house are typical of Green's stories: unpleasant people with ill-looking bodies and crabbed souls. His only communication is with the aunt, who is virtually estranged from her reclusive husband and spends hours telling young O'Donovan hair-raising tales of superstition and violence. She tells him of curses laid on people she has known, and when she speaks of the Scriptures it is only to relate the most terrifying passages.

The boy, understandably, distrusts his aunt and uncle and resolves to escape. His opportunity comes when he receives a gift of money that will enable him to attend the state university. But before he leaves home, he takes a walk to the local cemetery, whose beauty and peace always attracted him (in Green's stories cemeteries are one of the "special places" where unusual things happen). While he is there he is approached by a stranger whose appearance disturbs him, so he returns to his room. When he arrives at the university, a short time later, he is again approached by a stranger, who seems both mysterious and familiar to the boy. This time they engage in conversation, and the stranger, named Paul, accompanies Daniel as he goes to talk to the landlady of a roominghouse. Paul talks a good deal when alone with Daniel, but he is noticeably silent during the discussion with the landlady.

When the stranger departs, leaving Daniel alone in his new room with his books (*Frankenstein,* Byron's *The Vampire,* Hawthorne's novels, translations from the French), Daniel lapses into one of his frequent fits of melancholy. The stranger Paul returns at intervals, like an apparition, and confides the details of his life to Daniel. Paul, oddly enough, seems embarrassed at having no sins to relate. During the next few days Daniel has a recurring dream. It involves the "doubling" of himself, as he himself sees it. And when he awakens he finds himself compulsively driven to writing in a journal—the manuscript we are currently reading. He has a strong sense of being controlled by some outside force; he is no longer in charge, and he feels that somehow he is being pursued. When he takes walks around the campus he thinks he is covering the same terrain that appears in his dreams.

On one of these walks he talks with the campus minister, mostly about "heretical books" and purgative fire, and when he returns to his room, he finds that Paul has burned all his cherished books. He is furious and aggrieved, and he suddenly realizes something that had already occurred to the reader—that Paul is the stranger who approached him near the cemetery near his home. At this point the first manuscript ends.

In the second part of the manuscript, which picks up two days later, the stranger Paul appears in an increasingly peculiar light. Daniel sees Paul's face in the mirror when he is not there, and Paul reveals that he knows Daniel's innermost thoughts. Daniel decides that his melancholy and despair stem from his excessive attachment to things of this world, so in a frenzied state of mind, he renounces the material world, all its goods and attractions, and his hopes for earthly happiness. He collapses in a faint and awakens to find a letter from Paul, announcing the coming of "someone strong" who will protect and guide Daniel, if he will not resist him. The manuscript ends on that note.

The story then becomes a series of letters from various persons in a position to watch and judge Daniel. A letter from his uncle reveals that Daniel's parents were the victims of mental illness. His mother had gone insane; his father had been "melancholic" and had died at the age of forty (Daniel often suffers from sharp pains in his head). A letter from the landlady says that Daniel came alone on his first visit to her roominghouse—there was no Paul. She herself had burned his books, carrying out what she had understood to be his own wishes. She comments on his tendency to talk to himself, sometimes in a strangely altered voice.

A Doctor Thornton, who had observed Daniel at the roominghouse, stresses Daniel's odd appearance and facial expressions, crafty and evasive, his abstracted and agitated manner, and his tendency to walk like an automaton. He recalls a young woman at the dining table commenting about Daniel's having fallen into "hands more powerful than ours."

A letter from the sister of the clergyman Daniel had talked to on campus cites her brother's opinion: Daniel's "attack" was a "touch of grace" which converts the gentle by persuasion but strikes down the proud and the violent. Thus, she says, Daniel's death was a sign of either divine wisdom or human madness, depending on how you looked at it. She states flatly that Daniel's friend Paul was the "creation of a disordered mind," that the letter Daniel got from Paul was written by himself, a

case of automatic writing, and she ends her letter remarking on
the "psychological basis" of the "ugly story."

The story, then, stresses derangement as the source of Daniel's troubles. The major evidence, from his family heritage and
early boyhood experiences through to the letters stressing his
odd behavior, makes it apparent that Daniel was impelled by
the "someone strong" who was to "protect and guide him" to
throw himself to his death in the rocky ravine; that he was,
in short, the victim of his own disordered mind. Yet the possibility that Daniel was somehow guided by an alter ego who
was his better self (who had "no sins to confess"), a better self
closely identified with the Christian spiritual world (the burning of "bad" books and renouncing the material world)—this
possibility cannot be dismissed, despite all the "scientific" evidence. Or at least, Green could not dismiss it. He will return
to this theme and explore it in many different ways, though the
basic story will always remain ambiguous. As Green himself has
said, he is continually telling the same story, as if to discover
for himself where its real truth lies.

IV   The Keys of Death

In *The Keys of Death* (*Les Clefs de la Mort*)[8] the story opens
also with the romantic Poe-like device of an old manuscript discovered in the desk in an ancient house. The discoverer of the
manuscript (he calls himself only R. N.) feels an urge to "complete the manuscript." Thus the story is in two parts—the original MS, dated 1910, and the completed MS, dated 1925. The
story begins, then, in 1910, after the narrator's introduction relating how he came into posssesion of the manuscript.

The scene presents the writer of the first MS, named John,
lying amidst tall grass and flowers listening to the sounds and
song of a reaper working nearby. John is an ardent young man
of frustrated and unattainable desires, who often has recourse
to nature as source of solace. In this scene, the grass was "still
thick and still full of those fragile flowers without perfume which
live but a few days in the wind and sun. They bent over my
face as if they were trying to hide me from the reaper, but at
the slightest breathe of air they swayed and waved about in
all directions." The flowers suggest the comforting and protective

fertility of nature. (But, as we will see, they are ultimately help-less before the other aspects of nature hostile to them. The sun and wind are usually negative elements in Green.)

Soon the voice of the reaper and his song are replaced by a mysterious "other voice"—not traceable to the wind or anything tangible. "It resembled no human voice nor any other sound which I have ever heard." It seemed to rise in protest and op-position to the human voice of the reaper. But when the reaper himself appears, a huge silhouette against the sky, the "other voice" is dispelled—for the time being.

The narrative now shifts to the present tense, and we are intro-duced into the familiar Greenian family situation: the child with one parent in a large old house. The boy feels detached from the mother whose days are taken up entirely with the routine trivia of household duties which never vary through the years, and, in his loneliness, he is given to strange experiences of alienation from ordinary "reality." John is struck by the fan-tastic unreality of his mother and her maid—they appear as a ghostly vision, moving trancelike through their routine gestures. The boy slips out of the dark and oppressive house and hides in a shadowy clump of trees where in years past he played with his second-cousin Odile. Wind, lightning, and time have dam-aged the old trees, but they still offer a sense of sanctuary, and in their midst John waits the return of Odile, who is coming home, ill, from the city where she has been staying.

The manuscript breaks off, and the next section begins (the second "completed" manuscript dated 1925) with a retrospec-tive survey of John's childhood relations with Odile and the games they played under the detached eye of the mother. In one scene the two children are alone in a room and studying the figures in a Persian carpet, figures representing animals with men hunting them. There was, related John, "something savage and sacred in the ancient Oriental design which pleased me so." But Odile insists that the figures in the carpet were hunting *them*, not the animals—"the eyes are fixed on us"—only, she added, "they are not real people." She was a "strange little girl," thinks John, "with a precocious determination to withhold herself from the world's scrutiny." This strange little girl, of mysterious ori-gins, will prove to have a remarkable sense of the unseen menace that will threaten John. He does not understand Odile, yet he

feels close to her, a sense of rapport which is to fade as they
grow into their teens and especially after the appearance on the
scene of Jalon. Jalon, unremarkable yet somehow sinister in
his appearance, comes to the family as a distant relative, and by
means of blackmail proceeds to take over the household. From
the first he makes a profound yet unaccountable impression on
the young John. Jalon's portly figure is contrasted with the tiny
and timid mother who stands in great awe of him. John develops
a strong hostility to the intruder, especially as he himself loses
rapport with Odile (they are now fifteen and thirteen, respec-
tively). John senses a kind of "complicity" between Jalon and
the girl which he cannot understand.

In one of the central episodes John experiences a violent yet
trancelike reaction to seeing Odile and Jalon approach each
other familiarly. His suppressed desire for the girl and strong
feelings of possession overwhelm him—blood pounds through
his veins and he feels himself transported outside time and space.
The other two are transfigured, in his eyes, into dream figures
existing on some other level of being. John loses consciousness
and is ill, as a consequence, for a few months. He emerges from
his convalescence a changed person. He went to bed a child
and arises a man, but his change is characterized primarily by
his decision to assert himself against the intruder. He decides to
murder Jalon. He soon develops the strange mental state of the
would-be killer, the strong sense of having a "double"—an
"invisible being" which has moved inside him and governs him.
He is no longer master of himself. But one of the most curious
results is that, with the growth of his resolve to kill Jalon, his
hatred for his intended victim diminishes. John is now the "complete assassin" in every respect except for the act itself, which
has become almost irrelevant. On the surface nothing has
changed, but in reality everything has changed. John is now on
"good terms" with his intended victim; he even experiences a
form of happiness. But he responds and acts entirely in accord-
ance with an "inner voice," and it notifies him when and where
the murder of Jalon is to take place. However, when he enters
Jalon's room on the appointed night, and at the very moment
when the murder is to occur, the voice suddenly deserts him.
Months of dominance by the "invisible being" and "inner voice"

drop away, and John is back where he started, irresolute and frightened. He flees from Jalon's room.

The story has now come full circle, and we are given a rerun of the opening pages of the first manuscript: the episode in the meadow with the reaper's song. John now recognizes the strange, pervasive "voice" as his own, and it is terrifying in its intensity. This time the reaper's song does not dispell the voice, and it returns to urge once again the murder of Jalon. Later, John leaves his room to go to Jalon's but instead he finds himself moving compulsively toward Odile's (she had said previously that he would come to her on this day). The sick girl reveals to John that she had known of his intentions. She then is overcome by a kind of delirium, and, claiming that she sees a "black man" in the trees outside the house, she dies.

John now understands that Odile, having "known," had prevented him from killing Jalon. She had exerted a spiritual counterforce to the murderous "voice"—John had summoned death, and she had chosen to be herself its victim, because death would not depart empty-handed. At her funeral, John finds himself gazing fixedly at the crucifix on her coffin. We are given the strong impression that Christianity, in some inexplicable way, has triumphed over the forces of darkness and death.

Green's story, however, was written during the time of his estrangement from the Church, and it depicts a character who, like Denis in *L'Autre Sommeil,* professes to be a nonbeliever. But both these stories, while scarcely presenting an orthodox view of religion, are pervaded with a mystical and religious atmosphere. Green says in his *Journal*: "I was preserved from atheism just as I was spared crawling on all fours and cropping grass. . . . The idea that God might not exist has never so much touched me."[9] This story seems to presage Green's ultimate return to the Church, whose faith he had never really abandoned, but at this stage in his religious development it appears that death is not to be denied—it claims its victim—and the role of the crucifix shining on the coffin remains in doubt.

Green began writing this obscure narrative after the death of his father (July 1, 1927), which explains in part the general tone of the story as well as the original title *Azraël* (the Moslem angel of death).[10] He changed the title to *The Keys of Death,* which is derived from the Bible—Revelations 1:18 (in French texts, "Revelation" is called "Apocalypse," which is the Greek word for revelation and also carries the meaning of "obscure allegory"). In the biblical story a revelation came to Saint John in the form of a vision of the future of Christianity and its final triumph after the reign of the Anti-Christ, and it is the implied parallel between the experiences of the two Johns that supports the suggestion of eventual triumph over death, the black specter in the trees seen by the dying Odile (also the name of a saint) as she sacrifices herself for John.

CHAPTER 3

Journeys to Nowhere: The First Novels

I Avarice House

GREEN'S first full-length novel, *Avarice House* (*Mont-Cinère*, 1926, 1927),[1] contains and foreshadows the technique and many of the themes to be developed in his later works. This story, like those to follow, is a study of obsession. Kate Fletcher, the mother of the central character, Emily, is the complete miser, her miserliness taking the form of obsessive "economizing," supported by habits of hypocrisy, cowardice, suspiciousness, devotion to trivial busiwork. Known by the townsfolk as a "good woman," her façade of pleasant and amiable meekness disguises her underlying tendency to violence and viciousness. Her disposition runs to extremes—from timorous withdrawal to explosive verbal assault. As with most of Green's characters, the mother's nature has been formed by her past, by early years of poverty which narrowed and cramped her character. Kate Fletcher's own mother, having been raised amid wealth and gracious living, had adopted strict economy measures as a distasteful necessity. With Kate it had become an obsession for *money* and with Kate's daughter Emily it had taken a still different form: desire for exclusive possession of *things*. Hence, three forms of "avarice" are handed down with increasing intensity through three generations. Kate Fletcher, formed by poverty, remains niggardly even after her marriage which provides temporary affluence: "powerless to master old habits, she resolved to return to them and to carry on her life in the channel which seemed to suit her best." Overruling all contrary instincts, "she was a woman in arms against herself, and there was an almost ascetic quality to her determined renunciation." She sees all objects and persons in terms of what they cost, what they will sell for. She has no sense of intrinsic value. She devotes most of her mental activity to devising schemes for "economizing"—translating objects into cash, buying at bargain prices (being blind to true value, she usually buys junk—her bargains are not really bargains), and the money she acquires she hoards. Toward the end of the story her money in the bank becomes an instrument of power, her ace in the hole. Emily, on the other hand, wants *things*, not money. She values things in and for themselves. She takes pride and pleasure in *possession*, in ownership, and this in turn becomes associated with power: the ever-present question of who is going to make the decisions.

The demands made on the mother are almost exclusively financial: the penurious Stephenses ask for neighborly handouts; the Church, in the form of the Reverend Sedgwick, requests donations; and ultimately her daughter and new husband demand a share in the mother's bank hoardings in order to pay off a small mountain of bills. None of these demands, needless to say, is honored. In this area alone—her bank account—Mrs. Fletcher stands fast; in others, she could be cowed and driven. And, from her own standpoint, she is right; in the end she is victorious. She leaves the doomed house, free and unencumbered, to start a new life, only because she has held on to her ace card—her money.

The daughter Emily, "silent and self-contained," is first seen as a totally negative character—solitary, unloved, unlovely, passive, and subservient to her mother. But she gradually grows in strength of character to the point where she can challenge and overthrow her tyrannical mother. But growth in moral strength is born of growth in obsessive passion—the determination to inherit *all* of Ashley House, the family home. Ashley House is her only "love," the only object of emotional concern, and she is increasingly impatient to have it for her own. And except for a passing response to the maleness of Reverend Sedgwick, her obsession drives out all other emotions except hatred for her mother and hostility toward all who might threaten her ultimate possession of Ashley House.

Emily's passion for *exclusive* possession ultimately ruins her: her hostility toward "intruders," first the boarder Miss Gay, then Frank and his daughter by a previous marriage (a mere baby), is what triggers the eruption that results in final violence, madness, and self-destruction. The irony of this is, among other things, that Emily's worship of material things is a defense against time and decay, against those incessant reminders of the horror of disease and death in their physical aspects. The hideous deaths of her father and grandmother haunt Emily and are unconsciously related to her passion for *keeping things*. Things represent permanence, stability, resistance to time and change.

However, *"plus ça change. . . ."* The impossibility of real change is stressed throughout the novel, usually at the beginning of a chapter when the previous one had seemed to promise a meaningful change in persons' destinies. Rather, we see destiny at work, reasserting itself, relentless and inescapable. Chapter 41 begins: "It was astonishing how few changes Emily's marriage wrought in the life at Ashley House"; and Chapter 44 begins: "In actual fact the little girl [Frank's daughter] brought very few changes to the way of life at Ashley House." But the important thing here is that Emily does not really want change, she does not want to escape or to alter life. She wants no change except in the domestic power structure and in local comforts of living (fires and warm clothes); she resists her mother's attempts to change the status quo by selling the family possessions and taking in boarders. Emily wants possession in order that time and change can be resisted. Hence, her insistence on inheriting, intact, her father's things is the only form of stability available, a sort of father surrogate.

Emily's grandmother, Mrs. Eliot, the mother of Kate Fletcher, completes this obsessed triumvirate. Her arrival on the scene, her moving into Ashley House as star boarder, not only completes the three-generation study of avarice, but provides a structural parallelism within the story: the mutual fear and hatred between Mrs. Eliot and her daughter Kate, and between Kate and her daughter Emily. And when the eldest and the youngest join forces against the middle, the circle of the family fatality is closed. Within this self-contained arena of conflicting passions, the destinies of the three unhappy women are worked out in terms of recurrent and insistent motifs which provide the substance of the study: avarice, change, time, habit, ennui, silence, rooms, sex, and fire.

Time: Time drags, hangs heavy, throughout the story, especially in view of Emily's impatience to achieve her majority and take over the house. Time takes the form of long hours and days of *ennui*, interrupted only by violent emotional spasms. Hatred, anger, and frustrated desire are the only real human emotions, but at least they help to combat ennui. But ennui is ably served by that most bourgeois of characteristics—routine. Almost the sole daily activities are reading and sewing, endless sewing. For related to the elements of time and change is the role of *habit*. Habit, or custom, from Proust to Camus, is a dominant human vice in modern literature, and it finds its place in the work of Green. But it is also a form of security and a main source of continuity and coherence in human lives. It serves as protection against the disruptive force of the outer world, for once that force enters into placid lives, it breaks up habits and contributes to the destruction of people. So habit and custom are to an extent to be cherished by most persons, but they can also become responsible for the nonlife of the fearful bourgeoisie. Habit, which plays a role in the deadly life at Ashley House, will become Nemesis itself to Adrienne Mesurat in Green's second novel, *The Closed Garden*. And in *Avarice House*, one of the principal means of fighting routine and ennui is missing. Or rather it—sex— is present only in disguised, covert, and perverted form.

Sex: As already indicated, what might ordinarily be considered sexual/emotional inclinations are totally subsumed under the overwhelming emotions of greed and hatred. Except for Emily's passing interest in Reverend Sedgwick and some references to her having the "usual romantic dreams" and a fondness for novels —"foreign romances"—there is no mention of sex or of sexual interest. After the marriage of Frank and Emily, there are no intimacies, and Emily shows total ignorance of the processes of parenthood. She is sexually stunted, the passion for possession having driven out everything else. "Marriage is for other people," she thinks, when she thinks of it at all. For the most part it never enters her head, and it is particularly ironic that the good reverend should so completely misunderstand what he considers to be her "evil thoughts." The absence of sexuality in this novel is noteworthy in view of the centrality of sexual obsession in the later works.

Silence: The pervading atmosphere of the story is one of icy silence. The first words of the novel are "Emily was silent," and they serve to establish the nature of human relationship in the gloomy old house: noncommunication, nonrapport, in the solitary, solipsistic lives of mother and daughter. Emily had adopted the habit of silence from her dead father, who soon after his unhappy marriage, had discovered silence to be his principal weapon against his wife. It has become Emily's principal weapon against her mother, as it will become that of the man Emily eventually marries, Frank Stephens. Speech, when it does occur, takes a form of a tactic, a defense, an evasion, and never a link between two lonely human beings. For these people ordinary speech is, in fact, an audible form of silence. The only real alternative to silence is its gross opposite—the outbursts of shouting, invective, and searing recrimination which erupt not infrequently to shatter the deadly routine of estrangement. During these spasms of loud verbal abuse, the characters at least have the satisfaction of momentarily understanding each other. Otherwise, what ordinary speech there is results only in misunderstanding: between Emily and the Reverend Sedgwick, Emily and her near-friend Prudence, Emily and her husband Frank. The only real communication takes place between Emily and her grandmother Mrs. Eliot, and the setting is the most important place in the novel, the guest bedroom.

The Bedroom: In Green's novels rooms play significant roles. They have their own histories, almost their own personalities, which seem to exert a palpable pressure on the persons who inhabit them. In *Avarice House* the room most in evidence is the guest bedroom. It is the scene of the most important events in the novel: (1) the deaths of the father and grandmother occur there, providing graphic imagery of terrifying death motifs which run throughout Emily's mental existence; (2) the only "friendship" which Emily experiences develops there—the good-evil relationship with Mrs. Eliot, the grandmother who influences Emily so greatly and forms much of her character, her education, her values, and her objectives; (3) the first and crucial "victory" of Emily over her mother takes place there; (4) after the death of the father, whoever occupies the Bedroom dominates the house—grandmother, the next boarder Miss Gay, the husband Frank; (5) its fireplace possesses the only fire in the house outside of the kitchen stove, since one of the mother's main and, as it develops, fatal economies is to deny the comforts of fire to the rest of the household.

Fire: It is the persistent symbol of the good life, of comfort and well-being, of the warmth lacking in human relations. It

stands in sharp contrast to the pervasive coldness, physical and
emotional, of life at Ashley House, and it is in the presence of
the only fire, a very small fire, that Emily and her grandmother
establish a certain rapport. Emily's triumph over her mother will
take the concrete form of control of the key to the wood cellar
and of Emily's ecstatic building of fires in the living room. After
her victory over her mother, Emily presides over the new fires
ritualistically, like a primitive priestess, and in her subsequent
madness she succeeds in burning the house down, herself included. For all its naturalistic focus on the miserable lives of
inconsequential people, the story takes on symbolic and even
mythic overtones in the Promethean echoes of the fire imagery
and in the ultimate destruction of the prized Ashley House by
the very element which signified its total possession. For fire is
also the symbol of human passion which eats away and destroys
the life that feeds it.

In this connection it is interesting to consider the book's title,
Mont-Cinère: *"cinère"* suggesting its root *cinus* ("ashes"), related
to the French *cinéraire* and the English "cinerarium": "a place
to receive the ashes of the cremated dead," which in turn suggests
Ashley House, or, using the same initials, Avarice House.[2]

II   The Closed Garden

The Closed Garden (*Adrienne Mesurat*, 1927, 1928)[3] presents
a situation comparable in many ways to that of *Avarice House*: a
young girl living in a provincial house that is more a prison than
a home, the other inmates being a self-satisfied bourgeois father
who dominates Adrienne and her sickly sister Germaine. As
distinct from the ill-favored Emily of *Avarice House*, Adrienne
is beautiful, healthy, strong and suffers only from loneliness, which
is to some extent self-imposed. Like Emily, she is a victim of
emotional starvation, and having no normal outlets she fastens,
strictly by chance, on a neighboring doctor as object of her love.
Given to taking long solitary walks in the afternoons and evenings,
she sees the doctor only briefly, on one occasion, as he passes
in his carriage. He is a singularly unprepossessing man, but to
Adrienne, driven by largely unconscious desires, his maleness
presents itself to her with overwhelming force, and she falls in
love with this man, who is largely a creation of her imagination

and her longing to escape. He becomes an important element in her growing obsession to flee from her father's house. For all his middle-aged lack of romantic qualities, he becomes the romantic means to her salvation. Needless to say, for the bulk of the story he is scarcely aware of the girl's existence.

The novel is divided into three parts. The first portrays in depressing detail the humdrum and rigid lives of the Mesurat family, reveals Adrienne's growing desperation, and rises to a climax in the violence of the father's death. The second part depicts Adrienne's attempts at flight, her feverish escape to another town, culminating in nightmare and terror in a lonely hotel room. The third part describes Adrienne's return home, her attempts to find a life for herself, marked by a series of cruel traumatic experiences which lead her relentlessly to mental collapse and madness. The entire story reads like a bad dream, Adrienne's dream. The author draws a firm line around his characters and milieu, all thought and action being confined to Adrienne's sensibility, every sensation, every gesture being intensely focused and highlighted with merciless clarity—the clarity of nightmare and surrealistic vision. The narrative moves steadily from the humdrum commonplace toward fantasy and hallucination. Ordinary persons whom Adrienne meets become, to her, menacing and sinister figures. During her flight from home every hotel room becomes a scene of terror, of ghosts and visions, a prison cell from which she flees, only to find herself in another equally as oppressive. These forbidding hotels and oppressive rooms have a kind of Kafkaesque inevitability about them. She is incapable of finding a pleasant room in a congenial hotel filled with sympathetic people. For Adrienne, in her world, such do not exist.

It is a cruel story—the series of devastating experiences which befall the unhappy girl are the concoctions of a devilishly ingenious fatality. The woman who moves in across the street, Adrienne's confidante and the closest thing she has to a friend, turns out to be a conniving, immoral creature of marked sadistic tendencies, who enjoys her power over the helpless Adrienne. The doctor proves to be a confirmed bachelor for good reasons: he is ill and destined for a short life. When Adrienne finally lures him to her house on the pretense of being indisposed, and confesses, in near hysteria, her passion for him, he is shocked and dumbfounded.

He retreats in haste, explaining his own unsuitability as possible husband—having but few months to live—and leaves her a shattered heap on the floor. This he is forced to do, the situation being impossible, but he does so with tears in his eyes, the one gesture of human compassion (perhaps for himself as well as for the girl) in the entire story.

This is followed by visitations from the doctor's sister, with whom he lives: a granite-hard hawk of a woman, jealously protective of her brother, who attacks Adrienne with vicious verbal assault and threats. And she has something to threaten Adrienne with, for over all these frightening and abortive attempts to find a life for herself, to escape the prison of loneliness, hangs the specter of her father's death, which was, to an undetermined extent, Adrienne's fault. It was during a tussle at the top of the staircase, in the dark, that Adrienne contrived, or happened, to push her father. He was found dead on the tile floor the next morning, apparently the victim of an accidental fall. Adrienne is questioned but not charged. But she *knows,* her neighbor has guessed, and late in the story, when Adrienne has returned home from her abortive attempts to escape, and when she has suffered all the nervous shocks her mind is capable of sustaining, her maid lets her know that there is an increasing amount of unpleasant gossip about the town. So when she is told bluntly to get out of town by the doctor's irate sister, Adrienne makes her last attempt to escape. But she ends up wandering around the dark side streets, under the impression that she is indeed going somewhere, but she is, by now, totally insane.

In the case of Emily Fletcher of *Avarice House,* her fate was stamped all over her from the outset: she was undersized, sickly, uneducated, timorous, ugly, and prematurely aged. One is surprised only that she put up as good a struggle as she did. But in the case of Adrienne, the situation is entirely different. Adrienne, at the age of eighteen, is not only the opposite of Emily in appearance and general endowments, she is also a "strong" character, and it is the slow destruction of a strong person, one who is prepared to overcome all but the most monstrous obstacles, that gives the story its peculiar and horrible fascination.

The source of Adrienne's strength is set forth at the beginning, when we find her, on the opening page, viewing the "graveyard"— a group of family portraits on the wall: the aggressive, ruthless,

determined visages of the Mesurats, born "leaders," juxtaposed
with the easygoing vacant faces of the Lecuyers and Serres. All
are dominated by the portrait of the grandmother, Antoinette
Mesurat, a stubborn, energetic woman with a forehead "like a
wall." A few pages later Adrienne is called "a true Mesurat": she
has a "haughty expression" and a "passion for authority." She
resembles her grandmother, only with a more youthful bloom,
displaying an air of innocence on a face "where decision was the
dominant trait." She is dressed as a servant; she shows her physical strength by moving heavy furniture with ease; and she reveals
a tough-minded attitude toward the problems of her ailing sister.
"Everything in her that was morose and disdainful—the Mesurat
side of her character, in a word—had developed at the expense
of the Lecuyer." She possessed the severity, the "concentration
and firmness," of her paternal heritage. She had no friends and
desired none: "Nothing seemed to influence her. She feared nothing, desired nothing. Boredom and a sort of sullen resignation
could alone be read upon her face."

The cause of her boredom is obvious enough, for the role of
habit, in this story as in *Avarice House,* is paramount. Life for
the Mesurats had become a series of habits, of fixed gestures ac-
complished at fixed moments. Change of any sort, in the Mesurat
household, would have "worn the air of anarchy." There had been
no "events" in Adrienne's life, either good or bad, and, as in the
more understandable case of Emily Fletcher, no thought of marriage occurred to her, or to anyone else in the family. She had had
local suitors but had rejected them all, for they offered not escape
or enrichment of life but an extension and continuation of her
present existence—of her present round of routine.

As a rule in Green's stories, habit and its inevitable offspring,
ennui, are products of enclosed places, where everything seems
stable, for everything is fixed. Fixed habits become synonymous
with walls, rooms, and houses. Adrienne is a victim of habits
unchanged even by the death of her father: "From her father
she had inherited a sort of habitual veneration which kept her
inside these walls." She knows she can never leave her father's
house. She is controlled by a past which has become tyrannical.
When empty of content, habits are gestures which have lost all
relationship to the meaning they formerly had. "She had come
to resemble a religious whose faith has been lost, yet who keeps

a sort of irritable attachment for her rule because it is the rule which she once chose for herself."

In a similar fashion, habits govern Aunt Rose in Green's later novel, *Midnight*: while repeating the story of death of relatives, she is obsessed with a clean kitchen, which she scrubs incessantly even though nobody soils it any more. Her endlessly repeated gestures, acts, and recitations have lost their original substance. They express a past which survives only in remnants and is unintegrated with the present, and they dominate and stifle instead of preserving the past in any true sense of continuity. But in the case of Adrienne, under the façade of resignation to a monotonous routine there simmers a great restlessness, unsuspected by others, and to some extent by herself. And this restlessness will seek direction, an outlet, an object; it will develop into obsession even before it becomes a conscious force.

This, then, is the solid young lady that fate must subdue, a fate that appears first in the form of her father, a retired bourgeois, aged sixty, complacent and content in his bovine way. He is jovial and tyrannical at home, but, like Emily's mother in *Avarice House,* is "timid as a child" outside his home. He has lived "beyond emotion" for years, he avoids disturbances, cherishes tranquillity, and has a ready smile, vacant eyes, and voluble speech. Absolute in his control at home, he is disturbed by his daughter Adrienne's strange nocturnal wanderings, especially when she denies to her father that she has even been outside. It is during one of these outings that Adrienne has her single overwhelming view of the doctor, but she keeps her infatuation a guarded secret, refusing to confess the reason for her strange behavior to her father and sister. They conspire to extract her secret, while on her side Adrienne conspires to have her sister's bedroom, as it affords a good view of the doctor's house. The father takes to locking the garden gate, making Adrienne a virtual prisoner ("the closed garden").

In a particularly brutal scene, a family card game in which Adrienne is emotionally incapable of participating, her mind and senses being in a state of numbed confusion, the father and sister succeed in forcing Adrienne, by combined verbal and physical harassment, to admit that she is in love. But she steadfastly refuses to name the man. This stark scene, a nightmarish episode of horror and unreality for Adrienne, introduces the

notion of possible madness, of madness as her ultimate fate. The
notion recurs a number of times as an ominous motif throughout
the story, as Adrienne is quite aware of the state of her mind.
During the card scene, when she finds herself incapable of gathering her thoughts and understanding the harsh directions
given her by her father, Adrienne wonders about her strange
condition: "It seemed to her that some unknown influence had
entered into the room she knew so well. An indefinable change
had taken place. It was like one of those dreams in which the
dreamer finds himself in a spot which he knows he has never
seen, yet which appears familiar. To her first feeling of curiosity,
fright had succeeded—then terror at feeling herself unable to
fly, paralyzed and a prisoner. She wondered, as she threw a
glance around, whether she were not going mad."

There is no escape from the circle of fear closing in around
her. The days are compounded of physical fear and hatred of
her father, contempt for her sickly spinster sister, and indulgence
in her fantasy life regarding the doctor. Her nights, far from
providing respite from the tensions of the day, offer only another
dimension to her sufferings. She often wakes in the darkness and
is terrified by the unseen and unknown. On one occasion she
remembers a line from Racine she had learned as a child. Now
it comes back in full force: *"C'était pendant l'horreur d'une profonde nuit."* She thinks: "There is no word truer or more eloquent
than 'horror' to describe the hour or so which precedes dawn."

During the day her mind, under pressure of her intense dwelling on her hopeless love for the doctor, starts to play tricks on
her, to indulge in hallucinations which frighten her, as she is
fully aware of their implications. Once after an especially strong
hallucination, "she asked herself if, this time, she were not really
going mad." She starts watching herself in mirrors and is invariably distressed by what she sees. On one occasion it is a double
image of herself which, while suggesting an aberrant vision, also
represents the schizoid direction of her development. Another
time she sees her hair falling down over her face: "There was
something wild in her face that surprised herself." Later, following a jarring exchange with her sister Germaine, "She took her
head in her hands as though to stop the thoughts that were rend-
ing her. A sort of madness took possession of her at the thought
of how absolutely alone she was." Green himself observes that

there are "certain souls whom loneliness has marked for its own,
and who pass without transition from an empty existence to a
species of interior frenzy which subverts their reason." After an
especially frightening night, Adrienne sees quite clearly the fate
awaiting her: "Suddenly she was penetrated with a formless
terror. It was not, as just now, the horror of something prowling
about her, the feeling of being hunted: rather it was an ignoble
horror of herself, of her slightest gestures, of her shadow, even
of her thoughts, in which she believed she perceived the pre-
monitory symptoms of lunacy."

Thus Adrienne suffers from a special refinement of cruelty in
that she has full consciousness of what is happening to her while
her mind is in the process of disintegration, and she is powerless
to stem the process. But ironically, the "nothing was changing
in her life" becomes another recurrent phrase that passes through
her mind, though it takes on a peculiarly bitter cast, for she knows
well that everything has changed except the external form of
things. Her external life has become even more strictly routine
and circumscribed, while her inner life is becoming progressively
deranged. So ultimately she strikes out against the forces that
are suffocating her, but instead of achieving her liberation, she,
like Emily Fletcher, works toward her own defeat.

What makes this somber story so convincing, so hauntingly
real, in spite of the almost incredible consistency in the pattern
of mischance that engulfs the heroine, is Green's style, his mas-
tery of the art of giving substance and body to the atmosphere
which surrounds the characters and settings, of giving it such
density that to read it is to enter into a specialized and closed
world that becomes one's own world. One "lives" the life of the
novel, in spite of the unmistakably Gothic, indeed melodramatic,
nature of the tragic events. Green's art is directed toward intensi-
fication of human experience, and action is pushed beyond the
limits of common social experience. This aspect of his work has
caused certain critics to dismiss his novels as mere case studies
of psychosis, too remote from normal life to have any general
appeal. Such criticisms cannot be taken too seriously, of course,
since they would tend to eliminate from the shelf of great works
many of unquestionable power. Indeed it is Dostoevsky's Raskolnikov, the Brontë sisters' ill-fated heroines, Hawthorne's haunted
women, Hardy's star-crossed victims that come to mind when

one reads Green's tightly wrought dramas. Like these forebears
in the art of psychological trauma, Green creates a convincing
illusion of reality through his ability to "heighten the laws of circumstance against a commonplace background." Theme, characters, and setting are blended and balanced, and intense crises
of situation are modulated to a tone of realistic simplicity. While,
as in Kafka, the source of horror is sometimes inexplicable—
sleeping dream, hallucination, supernatural manifestations are
not always distinguishable—the horror is transmuted into accept-
able and intelligible human emotions.

It is a tribute to Green's art that the reader can be so totally
absorbed into the novel's actions, since it is a world that seems
to exist outside time and space as normally experienced. In both
Avarice House and *The Closed Garden* the stories are entirely
self-contained: only matters directly related to the relentless
processes of mental disintegration are included. There is no trace
of local color, of the humorous incidents that make up the daily
life of even the dreariest of provincial towns; there is not one
reference to any event outside the minds and manias of the central characters—the three Fletcher women in *Avarice House,* and
in *The Closed Garden,* the solitary mind of Adrienne. And within
that closed mental world, fates are worked out with the slow
logic of nightmare, each event, each response, growing inexor-
ably out of the previous one, with an overwhelming sense of inevitability. In this sense, Green's is truly a classic art.

III   The Dark Journey

Green's third novel, *The Dark Journey* (*Léviathan,* 1929),[4]
is similar to the first two in its "closed techniques." It is also a
"self-contained" drama in which the entire story is confined within the sensibilities of the immediate characters, and contacts with
the "outside world" are slight. But it differs in that it offers a
larger variety of life. There are several important characters, and
the action covers several locales. But there is one character whose
life begins and ends the novel and who provides the thread of
continuity that interrelates the lives of others. Paul Guéret receives the main focus, and his actions serve to illuminate the
lives and actions of other persons, whom he forces to confront
their own basic natures. In so doing he brings violence and disas-

ter on most of the people who become involved with him. Paul
Guéret is a somber, hulking man somewhere in his thirties, un-
happily married to a retiring woman who plays no part whatever
in his life. Guéret is infatuated with an attractive young woman,
Angèle, who works in a dubious capacity for Madame Londe,
imperious proprietress of the town's principal café. Guéret is persistent but uniformly unsuccessful in his pursuit of Angèle, who
leads him on but grants him none of the favors she so evidently
grants to others—that is, to the clientele of Madame Londe's café.

While the action of the story is primarily psychological in its
slow depiction of Guéret's developing obsession for Angèle, of his
increasing desperation and frantic determination to have the
young woman accept him as a lover, it erupts into violent action
on several occasions. First, when he manages, after a prolonged
and agonized struggle, to scale a high wall and gain entrance
into Angèle's bedroom, only to find that she has spent the night
elsewhere. And later, when driven by Angèle's provocations to
the point of mental derangement, he attacks her and leaves her
for dead on a river bank. In a state of delirium he flees, strikes
down an old man who gets in his path, and, in a vividly described
scene, hides in a moonlit coalyard for a night. He disappears for
a time, then returns to hover about the town, skulking around in
the darkness looking for Angèle, whom, as it turns out, he has
not killed but has disfigured for life. He is given sanctuary in the
house of the bored and frustrated Madame Grosgeorges until she
finally betrays him to the police.

In the course of this somber narrative the point of view alternates among several characters, each of whom reveals to us a
private world of unappeased and obsessive passions. As in Green's
other novels, each character is dominated by a single ruling passion which governs his life and determines his fate: "One passion
is enough for each person." Guéret is animated solely by physical
desire. Madame Londe, who presides despotically over her café
and its humble bourgeois clientele, is driven by love of power
fed by curiosity and desire for knowledge of the intimate affairs
of her customers. The beautiful Angèle, whose unsavory job it
is to extract private information from those clients by offering
herself in exchange for the gossipy details that her employer,
Madame Londe, cannot seem to live without, is obsessed by the
dream of escape from her humiliating life to one of true love

and romance with some young man her own age. With her middle-aged clients she experiences a routine of sexuality without love or pleasure, and one of the few enjoyments she has is playing a cat-and-mouse game with the impassioned Guéret. Madame Grosgeorges, wife of a complacent and overfed bourgeois, is the embodiment of boredom. Imprisoned in a fine house with her gross husband and unloved son, her only emotions are a longing to escape, a hatred which reveals itself in a sadistic treatment of her young boy, and a savage hostility to everything and everybody around her. Only Monsieur Grosgeorges seems "happy," for he is an insensitive and unrepressed bundle of appetites which are easily satisfied. Food and sex, his only interests, he comes by readily, and, lacking anything that could be called true passion, he is "content."

Guéret's obsession is, in a sense, the most "normal." This hulking man, inept and unattractive, is possessed by a not unusual desire for a pretty young girl, but it is his peculiar fate to do and say everything that would alienate the object of his love and never do the right thing which to someone else would have been natural and easy. His problem is that he is truly and hopelessly in love, which ironically makes him act the fool. Later in the story, Angèle begins to sense the value, the rareness, of Guéret's love in her loveless world, but then it is too late.

Guéret and Madame Grosgeorges can be seen as counterparts in many ways; they are both parallel and opposite. Both suffer from frustrated sexuality and hunger for love, Guéret consciously and Madame Grosgeorges unconsciously until her late awakening to the truth about herself. Both are subject to hallucinatory compulsions, repressions which erupt into violence, especially where sexual desire is involved: Guéret "kills" Angèle, and Madame "kills" Guéret, but only after discovering her unsuspected desire for him. The one is very humble and poor, and the other is haughty and rich; but they share basic weaknesses, and they experience a sense of complicity. Madame is surprised to discover her empathetic participation in Guéret's crime, and it is only when she turns Guéret over to the police and moves toward her own attempted suicide that she realizes that she has hated Angèle, not for the girl's affairs with her husband, but as a rival for Guéret. In her gathering of all gossip and avid reading of all newspaper descriptions of Guéret's crime, she becomes aware that she is much like the desperate man and shares most of his impulses and failings. Both are cruelly mismatched in marriage, and both hate their spouses, though their spouses are of opposite kinds. Guéret has no relations with his wife, and Madame Grosgeorges' capacity for sexual love was destroyed during the first weeks of her marriage by her husband's brutality. In her, brutality and violence have taken the place of normal feelings of love. But Green only gives hints and suggestions of the motives underlying actions. He rarely spells them out. The characters try to account for their actions, but their own versions are scarcely credible, and we are left to draw our own inferences.

The novel is to a large degree about "Fate." The words "fate," "fatality," and "destiny" recur throughout the story and are invoked at every important decision and action. Fate, or its equivalent, is consciously held by each character to be directly responsible for everything, for his misery and misfortunes. In Green's early short story, "Léviathan," it appears as the sea, vast and ominous, associated with solitude, ennui, despair, and death. Its role is similar in this novel by the same name, with the added element of destiny. It appears as an inescapable and sinister force underlying the lives of men, a ubiquitous presence that actively seeks to prevent happiness on this earth. Its role is mysterious and ambivalent. At times it seems no more than a scapegoat— weak characters blame their weaknesses and wretched lives on fate. It seems a convenient excuse for their personal failures. At other times it does indeed appear to dominate the novel and determine the lot of each character, weak and strong alike. Léviathan, as a monster which dwells unsuspected for the most part, below the surface of human actions, rises into view only infrequently and then can be clearly seen as capable of enormous damage. When it does appear, it takes the form of the individual passions and obsessions which dominate men and drive them to their destruction.

IV   The Strange River

Green's fourth novel, *The Strange River* (*Épaves*, 1932),[5] is the product of his resolve to depict characters totally different from those he had created up to that time. He decided to replace the murderers and suicides with characters hopelessly incapable of such extreme actions: mediocrities, failures, cowards, the "living dead." The initial instigation was, according to Green himself, his loathing for the idle rich, the complacent bourgeoisie.[6]

This novel, the only one to be situated in Paris, centers around the river Seine. Its dark, brooding presence is felt throughout the story; it is the scene of some of the crucial actions; it looms large in the protagonist's thoughts and rises to the level of a symbol of considerable power. There is little by way of physical action, however, the movement of the narrative being primarily psychological and emotional. Indeed, the "hero," Philip, is fatally incapable of action, and the actions of the other two people in this somber drama, his wife Henriette and his sister-in-law Eliane, are futile and self-defeating. Philip, through whose mind most of the story is told, is a vivid example of what Green calls "bourgeois fear."[7] Emotionally dead, he feels only apprehension—fear of suffering bodily harm, of growing fat, of losing his charming good looks, which are his only "love."

The story reveals, in slow-paced detail, a few weeks in the nonlife of a rich and handsome man for whom the world has no use. A totally superfluous man with nothing to do, he dwells entirely within himself, dotes upon himself. His wife's sister also dotes on him. Living in the same apartment with Philip and Henriette, Eliane develops a hopeless, secret passion for her worthless and charming brother-in-law, whereas the wife, having for some time despaired of any real relationship with her husband, has taken a lover, one who in most respects is the opposite of Philip. While in its broadest implications the story is a condemnation of the wealthy middle class, in its immediate focus it is a close study of an alienated man trying to discover who he is, what he is, with his success in that quest taking the form of discovery of his own baseness. The point of view of the story alternates between the three main characters and provides multiple views of several key episodes—"reruns," so to speak—each exclusive of the other and revealing ironic disparities between a character's own version of things and that provided by his associates. The story is structured, in typical Green fashion, around several recurring motifs: mirrors, dreams, darkness, walking, stairs, and, of course, the river.

In the opening scene Philip, out for one of his customary nocturnal walks, finds himself by the river, looking down from an embankment to the dark quai below, where a strange scene is being enacted. A shabby couple, man and woman, are engaged in an argument that promises to become violent. As Philip looks and listens to the harsh voices rising from the shadows, he is aware of the ominous nature of the setting. He is enveloped in the darkness, while leaning over a parapet gazing down into a murky chasm—an "abyss" where human conflict is being enacted—a world inhabited, at the moment, only by Philip and the two figures whose actions seem to take place for his benefit alone. He cannot explain his great interest in the arguing couple, but as they move along the quai bordering the black stream, he feels a compulsion to follow and observe, though this is contrary to his habitual "instinct of caution"—the "presence of misery" always impels him to retreat. As the woman is apparently being badly abused, he knows that he ought to intervene, but this inclination is quickly offset by fear: "the deserted, badly lit wharf was far too forbidding a place." The woman is obviously in danger of being thrown into the Seine, and seeing Philip, she cries out to him. He hesitates, powerless to move. "Possibly at that moment he saw himself as he really was for the first time in his life." He turns and flees.

Back at the apartment, the point of view shifts to Eliane. We see her doting on Philip with uncritical and self-effacing deference. Cozily ensconced in the cloistered, stuffy security and "perfection" of the apartment, both Philip and Eliane spend considerable time watching themselves in mirrors, Philip with self-satisfaction tinged with apprehension over the possibility of finding some imperfection in a countenance that so far has escaped the effects of time, Eliane revealing her half-conscious but repressed obsession for her brother-in-law, a passion which will grow both in its intensity and in her awareness of it.

When Philip goes out again (it is his only activity—he is always going out), he goes into a world of dark, forbidding buildings; of long, empty streets; of numerous long flights of steps and embankments. He turns, compulsively, toward the river. There is a flashback to the preceding scene in the apartment, a rerun from Philip's point of view, affording a deeper view of his struggle with remorse over his failure of nerve, his failure to aid the threatened woman. Self-justification alternates with self-recrimi-

nation, with a growing dismay that will pervade his consciousness for the rest of the story. When his attentions return to the
river, now seen as a "black abyss, deep as the ocean," he indulges
in reflections, inspired by the presence of that dark, immutable,
ever-flowing stream, on the absurdity of civilization, of the human
condition, of his slavery to conformity and routine. Philip, for all
his weakness, is not imperceptive. He has a philosophical turn of
mind, and, in his long solitary walks, he is much given to contem-
plating human existence and his own inconsequential role in it.
He recognizes that he has never done anything as a free man:
"Like every one else, he was a slave of chance." A weak rationalization, he knows. He often ponders his own childhood, and
indulges in brooding recollections:

His whole being was always trying to realise itself elsewhere than
in the present. Someone, something changeless within him, resisted
the transformation of the years, a mysterious person without youth
or age, always the same, hidden in the depth of the eyes of the
dreamy child, and of a man wizened by age, a person whose queer
ego was almost a stranger to himself. This evening, beside the river,
he was keenly conscious of all that was inaccessible in the depth of
his own heart. How could he hope not to be lonely if he remained
a stranger even to himself? In this world, the end and object of
which we cannot understand, each one of us blindly follows a
secret destiny which he will perhaps never realise.

In his extreme alienation from the city and its people, Philip
has an overwhelming sense of unreality. He is only playacting at
life. His long efforts over the years to build an image of himself
(his preoccupation with mirrors) were all shattered in a moment's experience: his discovery of his true inescapable self, his
recognition of cowardice as his instinctual reaction to life's challenge. He alleviates his anguish for a moment by some sardonic
reflection on the gross irrelevance of courage to success in modern
middle-class life, but the anguish returns and is presently reinforced by another scene which serves to further solidify his new
conception of himself.

During one of his nocturnal walks, Philip is boldly approached
by a man, smaller than himself, who, without displaying a weapon,
demands money. Philip briefly considers resistance, then yields,
giving the man the contents of his wallet. The implications of
this robbery episode, while further revealing Philip's cowardice,

are different from those of the threatened woman. In the case of the woman there was a certain distance, both physical and moral, between Philip and his challenge. While he was physically afraid, the demands made on him were prephysical, so to speak, essentially moral, and allowed for a certain rationalization on his part following his failure to act. After all, he did not know the couple, and in a sense, it was none of his business. But the robbery was inescapably his business. The confrontation was personal, immediate. The robber established his superiority by his physical presence and by the mere threat of violence. Philip's cowardice in this instance is unmistakable, and he must acknowledge it.

One of the immediate results of this encounter is an enhancing of his tendency toward self-alienation, toward a *dédoublement*, the urge to escape from or at least stand apart from and observe himself. On his return to his apartment, he indulges in a strange reconstruction of the robbery episode, this time from the robber's point of view. Philip projects himself into the role of the robber and imagines how the scene must have appeared to him. He tries to see himself clearly as the other man must have seen him. He is struck by the futility of careful cultivation of body and mind when such cultivation fails to perform meaningfully in a crisis. Philip recognizes that he has lost his habitual sense of superiority to the common herd. He recognizes, in fact, his inherent inferiority—he is a man lacking the courage of the lower species. He regards himself in the mirror, noting the unmarked, characterless perfection of the youthful face, "smooth and empty as that of a statue." Part One of the story ends as Philip drops off to sleep, his last thoughts being of "my body . . . my body."

The first part of the story had begun *in medias res*, in intense and detailed immediacy. Part Two begins with a series of flashbacks revealing Philip's past: his fear of his stiff and highly moral father, his infatuation and marriage with Henriette, his impotence —his incapacity to have sexual relations with his wife. He could feel desire for his wife only when she was fully clothed. Then Eliane comes to live with them, to replace Henriette as wife, in a domestic, nonphysical sense. Henriette is gone most of the time, and Eliane dutifully keeps house.

The story enters a new phase with the arrival, home from boarding school, of Philip's son, a shy and unhappy boy carrying on the family tradition of fearing the cold and aloof father. There is a dreadful dinner scene in which Philip fails utterly to establish rapport with his son. The boy feels like an outsider in his own family. This dismal scene is counterpointed by recurrent references to a mirror in the dining room: both Philip and Eliane are constantly regarding their mirrored images, Philip for a specific reason. He is concerned to see if the image reveals his "secret." But no, the image is obligingly noncommittal. He preens himself mentally, then lapses into self-disgust when he realizes what he is doing.

The subsequent incident in the wine cellar is another setback for Philip's dwindling ego. In an effort to establish some kind of a relationship with his son, he tries to frighten the boy by sending him alone into the forbidding darkness of the cellar. He wishes to establish his superiority over the child and, even more, to drag the child down to his own level—to find cowardice in the boy which would make him his father's son. But the boy resolutely and unwaveringly fulfills his mission, thus establishing himself as "of another race." He seems to gaze steadily through his father and his façade. Philip, angered by his failure, would like to bully the boy, but he does not dare. Once again he consoles himself by considering his physical beauty, but he also wonders if moral taint could be reflected in physical decay. "Rather than see his body become disfigured he would have agreed to be twenty times as cowardly."

Philip does have one contact with the outside world. He plays the role of chairman of the board of an inherited business—a business he knows nothing whatever about. It bores him, it is unreal to him; and his monthly performance at board meetings is a farce. On one occasion, when he feels particularly useless and incompetent, he suddenly resigns. Throughout the entire long-winded session he has felt painfully uncomfortable, and his mind wanders incessantly. He begins to study his reflection in a great mirror in the conference room—or at least he tries to: he fails completely to find his image in the glass. "He looked desperately in the mirror for his own face, but a sort of mist began to float before his eyes. His hands gripped the edge of the table in an effort to recover his strength through contact with some hard, tough substance." He begins to address the group compulsively, babbling on as if in a trance. He abruptly announces his resigna-

tion and leaves the room. On his way home he studies himself
in the mirror in the taxi, which fascinates him far more than the
passing scenery. His own existence, his own identity and sense
of life, are constantly being threatened, and he must find reflected
evidence that he does in fact exist.

Philip's wife Henriette, who has been something of a minor
presence so far, seen entirely through the indifferent eyes of her
husband and the ambivalent eyes of her sister, occupies the center
of attention for a few important passages. We accompany her on
one of her visits to her lover, one Victor Tisserand, a shadowy
figure who represents Henriette's revolt against empty bourgeois
marriage. She is attracted to him precisely because he is ill-
favored, desperately poor, and lives in a most shabby fashion.
She is attracted by the sight and smell of poverty, reminiscent
of her youthful years when she and Eliane lived in happy destitu-
tion. In Victor's humble room she feels "alive"; she feels that only
there can she find "truth." But curiously enough, while Victor
represents in many ways the opposite of Philip, in certain important areas he is Philip's counterpart: he is a weak man, a
failure economically—he continually borrows money from Henriette in order to live. It would seem that in some obscure way
Henriette is attracted to weak and dependent men, and he does
serve as a source of revenge on Philip, who couldn't care less.

But, above all, Henriette's illicit affair, and the complicated
and devious route she takes to meet her lover, appealed to her
imagination and provided satisfactions denied her by her real
life. She would follow, in order to reach her lover's abode, a
complex "imaginary path" through the city streets, never varying
it one step to the right or left—it was part of a "strict ritual":

Like all people whom the world has not succeeded in making happy,
she sought within herself for the elements of her happiness. She
played at life the same way that children play at soldiers or brigands,
and nothing in her life seemed more real to her than this imaginary
path which cut across other people's paths, becoming sometimes
confused with them, now parting from them and joining them again,
but remaining, in spite of everything, quite distinct.

Philip's dim awareness of his role as cuckold is revealed during
his attendance at a movie which reproduces many features of his
own marriage. He senses a parallel between himself and the

deluded husband in the film, whose wife has been carrying on under his nose. When the husband discovers his wife with her lover, Philip "seemed to hear a voice crying from the depths of his heart and from the emptiness of his whole life, a strange voice that had to be forced back from his lips: 'Lucky man! He is going to suffer.'" Here Philip's insight is considerable. He grasps a central truth about himself: he not only cannot love, but he cannot feel real emotional pain. His feelings are entirely negative; he can feel only loss, absence of feeling, and nothing as positive as real suffering which would be a sign of his being truly alive.

While Philip's life drifts along on its plane of emotional anesthesia, Eliane's is becoming increasingly intense and desperate. Her deepening predicament—her growing awareness of her passion for Philip, a passion that, to her horror, she discovers to be carnal and sensual to an extent she never dreamed she was capable of. This physical desire is complicated by a new development: her growing contempt for Philip as a man. At the very time that she begins to see him as the hopeless and ineffectual man that he is, she accepts the knowledge of her equally hopeless desire for him, and she feels herself disintegrating under the tensions of her impossible predicament.

Following a long dream sequence, a nightmare of surrealistic horror in which she is fleeing through forbidding and foreign terrain, Eliane resolves her impossible situation by actually fleeing Philip's apartment, running off to an obscure boardinghouse to hide. But her long-pent-up emotions demand yet another outlet in the form of complete confession. She writes a letter to Philip confessing her passion for him and incidentally revealing the activities of Henriette and Victor. The letter of exposé has little effect. Philip has a detective follow Henriette, but nothing comes of the revelation of her affair. The only real "action" related to this episode is the spectacle of Eliane's gradual disintegration— her loss of dignity and sense of her own worth. Philip, weak and passive, has the power, by his mere existence, to destroy two women who, strangely enough, have opposite reactions to him. He is a passive catalytic agent, helpless to do anything voluntarily for or against the two women in his world.

Running through the story like a subterranean stream and occasionally rising to the surface is the problem of the murdered woman. For it turns out that in all probability she *was* murdered.

Philip has for weeks studied the daily news to see if anything had come of the woman who had cried out to him on the quai. Finally he does discover a small notice that the corpse of a woman has been found floating in the Seine a considerable distance downstream from where he had seen the couple. The body was bloated beyond recognition from having been many weeks in the water. There is no conclusive evidence that it is the same woman, but Philip is convinced that his failure to act on that fateful night had resulted in a murder which he could conceivably have prevented. His guilt is so intensified by this knowledge that he experiences a growing compulsion to confess, indirectly, to Eliane. She understands, which results in her increased contempt for him and in her increased sense of the degradation of her passion for him. It contributes directly to her resolve to write the letter of exposé, and to escape.

Another main development in the story is Philip's growing devotion to his son. Pallid as his emotions are, Philip's feeling for the boy is perhaps the only positive element in his character. He spends much time with his son, thinking that he sees his own reflection there—a reflection which for the first time is not his own image in a mirror. He sees himself in the boy in many ways but not in the essential one: the boy lacks the father's cowardice, which the father tests on several occasions. It is only by the river, in a tense scene where the boy is forced to approach closely and precariously to the running stream's edge, that the father finally sees fear in the boy's eyes. He feels closely drawn to his son, now that he has managed to establish what is, for him, the all-important common bond.

Associated with this developing sense of kinship with his son is Philip's ultimate acceptance of himself for what he really is. He used to imagine another self—one which he always hoped he might someday become, an ideal alter ego. He now recognizes that that other man, the man he might have been, does not exist.

There had been a time in his life at which the man he might have been was with him all day long. Philip used to be conscious of that strange presence and eagerly modeled his thoughts on that other man's, to the point of believing at last that a substitution had taken place, and he passed long years in great spiritual contentment. Then in the course of time a certain hour arrived in which the truth manifested itself, like the first far-off summons of death. The man he ought to be did not exist.

Philip returns to the river with his son. "By the river he remembered more things than he did in the streets." The dark stream becomes for him closely associated with the past: near the river "his memory spoke to him incessantly of what he had once been." He leaves the boy and goes to the river's edge: "All his life the river had attracted him without his being able to understand why. A sort of mysterious kinship existed between them." Sometimes he had the fleeting impression that the river was speaking to him, revealing its secrets. Yet it frightened him. The word "river" had also become associated, for him, with "suicide." But, he wonders, do rich and wealthy people kill themselves? Merely from boredom? Surely that is not enough—there must be some great sorrow or tragic event.

Yet the idea haunts him. Entertaining the idea of death raises him momentarily in his own estimation. Humiliated by his wasted life and by his lack of serious purpose, he thinks of suicide as the one worthy gesture. He feels a strong compulsion to touch the water. Trembling with fear, he bends precariously over and touches the river—first a finger, then the whole hand, then suddenly he seems no longer to be afraid. He rejoins his waiting son, and they walk off together to the sound of the "raucous shriek of a tug" on the river, the world's final comment on this abject man. But perhaps it is not the final comment. Philip has to some extent cracked out of his bourgeois shell; he has confronted and accepted his unflattering new image of himself; he has come to terms with the inscrutable and menacing river—the river of life and self—and he has found in his relations with his son a kind of redeeming love. To be sure, he is attracted by the reflection of himself in the boy, but it is nevertheless closer to unselfish love than anything he had ever experienced before, and, imperfect as the emotion might be, it is a movement toward authentic life.

Love, in Green's picture of the modern world, is usually reduced to a sense of possession and domination. Eliane observes: "That was what love meant—to belong to a man." Such possession leads to ennui and, instead of a sense of mutuality, to complete isolation. Eliane is isolated by passion from the object of her desire. That human love fails to dispel the solitude of man is one of Green's convictions, often observed in his *Journal*: "Nearly all of my characters are solitaries who cannot scale the wall that separates them from their fellows. 'Der Menschen Worte verstand ich nie. . . .' This verse of Hölderlin finds in me an extraordinary resonance." "The human being is separated from the rest of humanity by a barrier which almost never falls. . . . To speak to a man is to throw a bridge over an abyss, but is there, on the other side of the abyss, a road that prolongs the line of the bridge? Very rarely." Each man is wrapped in his own ego, a form of prison. Especially Philip, who is alienated from everyone around him: "Perhaps no one had ever known such perfect solitude as this man did in the heart of this over-peopled capital."

The world of the rich bourgeoisie, which Green detested, is a world of ennui. Speaking of *The Strange River*, Green has remarked in his *Journal*, "It was just like Philip to go and promenade his ennui in empty apartments," which corresponds to another entry in his *Journal*: "Lunched today at X's . . . in a funereal apartment where ennui crept about and roared. It was the bourgeois at his ease in his bourgeoisdom. . . . I let my hatred of the bourgeois burst out." Similiarly, in *The Dark Journey*, Madame Grosgeorges is trapped in "that frightful ennui which is the damnation of the rich."

The world of the rich bourgeoisie is a world of lies, but it can usually maintain an illusion of order and stability which protects its inmates from unexpected intrusions from the "outside." Philip hides his "intrusion," just as Adrienne Mesurat's father refused to acknowledge Germaine's sickness which would upset his routine and is furious at discovering that a man has entered Adrienne's life. Hence the drama of these novels stems from the explosion into violence of the orderly fake world of the bourgeois. The comforting order and habitual routine of characters living an "inauthentic life" is broken up by some intrusion from the outside world, often in the form of some unwelcome truth. The character is forced to confront himself, to see himself in a new light, and to accept a new truth. This acceptance might destroy him at the same time that it frees him from the prison of society and self in which he has been held captive. The escape from this prison begins at the precise point where a dialectic appears between the life of fixed habits and a disordered and disordering

element which upsets them.[8] Thus Philip, in *The Strange River*—
the circle of trivia that makes up his daily life is broken by his
unusual walk during which for the first time an appeal for
help is addressed to him by another person. And so he, whom
a singular destiny had sheltered from the world, is compelled
to consider the vanity of his experience: "yet several times this
evening he had felt himself seized upon by something real." His
exaggerated concern for himself had never led to a real knowledge of himself, for the mirrors in which the vain fellow loved
to regard himself did not reflect anything but an external image,
and it is only now when his self-contained world is invaded,
that he comes to know himself. "He felt suddenly dragged out
of himself and torn from the narrow groove of his peaceful
life." "For the first time in his life, perhaps, circumstances
brought him face to face with himself," and the whole "care-
fully erected structure" of his life was overthrown.

Likewise, Eliane discovers herself as the novel goes on. She
believed herself to be gentle and good, and gradually she discovered that she was "violent and unjust." And it is only toward
the end of the story, when Philip recounts his story in the third
person, as if it had happened to someone else, that she sees the
true character of the man she had known only by his external
appearances.

This compulsion, shared by Philip and Eliane, to try to discover their true identities in mirrors, had its counterpart in
Green's own life. In his autobiography one can find a number of
parallels between Green's experiences and Philip's, especially
in regard to narcissism and addiction to mirrors: "Since everything should be said (otherwise why write a book of this kind?)
I never saw a mirror without my heart leaping with joy, and
if I was alone I looked at myself lengthily and with passionate
interest . . . fascinated by the image I discovered, so it seemed
to me, on each occasion for the first time." And once, when his
mother said, "Your Uncle Willie was handsomer than you,"
Green was stung to the quick. "Handsomer than I! I asked myself seriously if that was possible, and I also asked it of my
mirror. What a monument of pride I was getting to be—without
in the least knowing it—under the cloak of great modesty . . .
my mirror reassured me."[9]

Similarly, Philip's mixed feelings of attraction and fear regarding the river was an important aspect of Green's own experience. He used to go and gaze for long periods at the Seine, "as though some sort of affinity existed between itself and me. While the sea disturbs and upsets me, I love the river that has flowed through my life. I must say that there was something dangerous about it to my mind and I was sensitive to that something. Simply by taking one step forward, you fell into those unfeeling depths and you died. For I did not know how to swim. 'Not too near the edge,' said my mother."[10]

Apart from the biographical parallels, it is tempting to consider this novel as, among other things, a modern version of the Narcissus myth.[11] While the theme is essentially that of the dehumanizing effects of modern bourgeois life, it bears notable resemblances to the earlier myth. The youth Narcissus, we recall, was irresistibly drawn to water. He saw in water what Philip saw in it: the mysterious source of life, the reflection of life flowing steadily and obscurely through time, and the reflection of the self. Narcissus was the son of the nymph Leirope, who had been ravished by a river-god who had entwined her in his coiling streams. The seer Teiresias had said to Narcissus' mother (in words which apply strikingly to Philip): "Narcissus will live to a ripe old age, provided that he never knows himself." But Narcissus' path becomes strewn with rejected lovers, including the nymph Echo, all of whom were attracted by his great beauty, of which he was very proud. He was ultimately destroyed by his love for his own image which he possessed but could not really possess. Echo (Eliane?), though rejected, remained enamored of him, but his only "true" love was himself. In the novel Philip comes to love his son—but, to a great extent, as another reflection of himself. Finally it is interesting to note that the flower narcissus was used for narcotic purposes, and the word came to mean "narcotic" or "benumbing"—terms that apply admirably to the description of Philip.

CHAPTER 4

World of Fantastic Night

ONE of the recurrent criticisms leveled at Green, especially during the socially minded 1930's, was that his work was too far removed from the life of the times: it failed to confront the issues of the day. An anonymous review, appearing in 1936, is typical: it asserts that Green is a consummate artist, comparable to Poe, but that his work lacks any imprint of the real world. His characters are unrelated to our time and place; they read no newspapers, they react to no forces operative in France —no news, no politics, no economic issues, no wars—no *life*. It is a pity, the critic states, that Green does not turn his great talents to the life that abounds around us, but he prefers to construct "an unreal, escapist midnight realm."[1]

This criticism is not inaccurate, and Green would have been the first to acknowledge it. He was fully aware of the untimely nature of his writing of that period. Speaking of the 1930's— *"les années terribles"*—he says that out of the tumult of those grim years arose a world in which he "could find no place." He could draw no material for a novel from the tragic years 1933-39. Gide had told him in December, 1936: "You are apolitical. Stay that way." But being "apolitical," or appearing to be, did not prevent him from feeling, increasingly each day, the horror of the approaching war. In the preface to the third volume of his *Journal,* he confesses: "I believe that I can say that all the books I have written since 1932 have been written with the after-thought that they should never be printed. . . . That illusion was the cause for my giving free rein to my fantasies, and I let myself go much more than I would have done in more tranquil times." It was in this frame of mind that *The Dreamer* and *Midnight* were written. However, in March, 1939, Green interrupted his journal; he no longer had any desire to write, he tells us, as soon as he became convinced that any kind of happiness was impossible to attain. Soon afterward, the storm

81

of war, which he had heard approaching for some time, broke about him.[2]

What actually happened to Green while he was writing his four novels of the 1930's is rather curious. The dualism of his character became intensified to the point where there seemed to be *two* Greens: one, the painter of reality; and the other, the explorer of the fantastic. The two Greens took turns, so to speak, each dominating the creative process to the exclusion of the other. To be sure, Green's "realism," rendered in such reassuring detail, always has a strong aura about it that evokes in the reader an increasing uneasiness. But in the novels of the 1930's the distinction between the two Greens is clearly discerned, and this authorial *dédoublement* is reflected in the unusual way in which two of the novels were written. The first ninety pages or so of *Midnight* are relatively realistic, but Green dropped the novel at that point and began an emphatically fantastic work—*The Dreamer*. The latter was written between the two parts of *Midnight*, for the author of *The Dreamer* returned, once that novel was completed, to finish *Midnight*. And it is obviously the second Green, the fantasist, who dominates throughout the second part of *Midnight* where the last 121 pages take us to Fontfroide, "a castle of mirages or a mirage of a castle—one doesn't know which."[3]

During the three years the author devoted to the two books (of which the second, *The Dreamer*, appeared first, in the spring of 1934, while *Midnight* was not published until March 1936), the second Green held sway over the first. He had found the magic key of escape and profited from it to explore unknown realms, and to penetrate ever further into the shadows in order to find a new voice, the voice which speaks of the Invisible World beyond. And it is this voice that is clearly heard in *The Dreamer*—a remarkable story that will be discussed in detail, as it is probably the best and most characteristic work of the "second Green."

I The Dreamer

The Dreamer (*Le Visionnaire*, 1934)[4] is built around two sets of characters, those belonging to the real world, and those created by one of the main characters in his fantasy life. The first group comprises Maria-Teresa, her domineering mother, and young cousin Manuel. The second group, conjured up by Manuel, includes Manuel himself, as he depicts himself in his journal, and two imaginary inhabitants of a neighboring castle: the Vicomtesse and the sinister Madame Georges. There are other characters, but they serve largely to provide actions and motifs for the illumination of the main characters.

Several themes provide the substance of the novel: reality and illusion, or life and dream; sex and religion, power, disease, and death. Maria-Teresa's story is related primarily to religion; her mother's to power (covertly related to sex and disease); and Manuel's to sex, religion, disease, and death. All three of these personages can find happiness only in some "visionary state," some form of escape from real life by means of imagination and illusion, though each to a different degree. The mother's vision is closest to this world, in which her desire to possess and control her nephew Manuel is transmuted into a "holy affection." Maria-Teresa's transitory devotion to religion and the nun's life is more an escape from mother and home rather than a true calling to the religious life; it is a vision of peace and beatitude that is misunderstood by the nuns. Manuel's is the true and complete vision—his escape into fantasy, while it lasts, is total, and "real life" is completely replaced by fantasy. The personages created by Manuel, and faithfully depicted in his journal, are essentially projections of his own obsession with disease and death and of the relationship of these dreaded entities with power and sex.

The story is divided into three parts told from two points of view, frequently interspersed with authorial comment. Part I, "Maria-Teresa's story," relates the religious-familial problems of a fourteen-year-old girl and her cousin Manuel, who has come to live with her and her mother. Part II, "Manuel's story," discloses the mixed reality-fantasy life of an ill-favored, unhappy boy, a few years older than Maria-Teresa, as he devises imaginary means of escaping from a life he finds intolerable. Part III, "Maria-Teresa's story (concluded)," depicts the return to "reality," the death of Manuel, and offers comments on the value of the "visionary life." All three stories are in first-person narrative, ostensibly, though there are evidences of the author's personal intrusion into the children's narratives. That is, he will occasionally include commentaries on such topics as religion and the role of imagination and brilliant diagnoses of character and personality, which obviously lie outside the range of his youthful narrators. These violations of the "purity" of the point of view are infrequent, however, and do not obtrude seriously into the story.

Part I introduces us, through the eyes of Maria-Teresa, to young Manuel and the fascination which a neighboring castle holds for the two children. It is presumably a real castle, but one that is enlivened and embroidered by the children's fancy. There are observations, in a significant foreshadowing, on Manuel's "vivid imagination" which enabled him constantly to add some strange new feature to the castle, and "it cannot have been very long before he conceived the idea of peopling it with persons of his own imagination . . . the fantastic building grew in all directions." In one of her frequent retrospective judgments, Maria-Teresa expresses her belief "that to some extent he believed the stories he told me and that he gradually fell under a kind of spell." But Maria-Teresa treats the whole thing as kind of a game, while it is apparent that Manuel lives seriously in a "world of illusion." She confesses that she was unaware that "this shy boy was looking for some secret exit from a world in which too many real things made him suffer . . . he longed for some sign of understanding from me."

There is a marked distinction between Manuel's real life, overridden with "diffidence and the fear of death grown out of all human proportion," and his fantasy life, where in "a universe in the likeness of his own radiant, awful, deep and secret nature, he cast off the burden of real life and seemed to recover his true stature." For Manuel, singularly lacking in natural endowment, is a most humble person: he is unpleasant in appearance, even ugly; he has been rejected by the army; his clothes are a shambles; he feels himself to be exceptionally commonplace in all respects; and he is morbidly self-conscious. But to complicate matters, he has developed a strong repressed sexual desire for his cousin, who looks two years older than her age, and Maria-Teresa, who is now turning fifteen, is losing sympathy with Manuel's world of fancy.

Maria-Teresa's situation is the familiar one in Green's fiction: an unloved child in a household dominated by a single parent.

The mother, according to her daughter's view, is cold and tyrannical. She is also dignified, handsome, severe, even awe-inspiring. Maria-Teresa is afraid of her, feels herself to be unloved, and fails to love her mother in return. The father has died, and when Manuel comes to live with them, the mother (his aunt) develops a surprising affection for him, an affection character-ized by extreme shifts in attitude—from open abuse of the young boy, who is scorned for his ugliness, to equally open love, of a sort, which takes the form of his aunt's lavishing attention on him. She is never happier than when Manuel is sick, for then this imperious woman can smother him in her maternal affections. She loves to dominate him and dictate to him, but she also likes to dress up for him, to attract his admiration. This complex and rather unhealthy relationship is clarified somewhat by the information that Manuel is the son of the man his aunt had wanted to marry. But his aunt's sister had won that man, now deceased, and his aunt had settled for a fatuous and humdrum military type, whose recent demise had gone un-lamented. The aunt's hostility for her sister was equaled by her desire for her sister's child, Manuel, the son of the man she had loved—a desire that is corrupted, often violently, by the fact that poor Manuel so obviously lacks the merits of his late father, for which his aunt can never forgive him. So she alter-nately berates and embraces him, and he comes to enjoy his periods of illness, when he can profit from his aunt's obsession. For since his own mother and father, along with his aunt's hus-band, had all died within the same year, he is now entirely in the possession of his aunt. In the physical sense, at least—in his fantasy life it is another matter.

One of the principal features of the novel is its treatment of religion, and while the views and judgments are ostensibly those of the youthful narrators, there is enough personal comment by the author to suggest that his narrators' views are also his own—at least at that particular time in his career. For example, when Maria-Teresa's mother is described as being "intensely reli-gious," Green observes: "I often wonder what sort of beasts we would become without a little religious hypocrisy to temper our evil instincts." This is said apropos of Maria-Teresa's mother, whose attitude toward her penurious sister, her contempt for her husband, her neurotic fixation on her nephew, all stand in grotesque contrast to her reputation as an "intensely religious" woman.

A similarly ironic tone dominates Green's portrayal of the two priests in the story and the account of young Maria-Teresa's brief affair with the good sisters at the Catholic school. Maria-Teresa, at the age of fourteen, is very religious and ignorant. She enjoys her days at the nun's school as a pleasant respite from her oppressive home life. She comes to love and envy the nuns and their tranquil lives. She is especially impressed with her tutor, the gentle Sister Louise, with her aura of self-sacrifice and otherworldliness. Maria-Teresa is unaware at that time that her intimacy with Sister Louise was arranged and encouraged by the Mother Superior: "she fell into the celestial trap laid for innocent souls." A "pious plot" had been woven around her; her need for love and attention and her devotion to the nuns and the nunnery as an escape from the harshness of her home life had been taken as signs of yearning after a religious life. Maria-Teresa thought so herself, and everyone's attitude toward her had changed. Sister Louise would smile and talk of purity of soul and the joys of the hereafter, and the young girl resolved to take the veil. But at home, when Maria-Teresa announces her intentions, her mother's reaction is very strange: total silence and a scowl. Maria-Teresa is perplexed, especially when on the next day her mother makes a visit to the convent to "straighten things out." This is followed by an atrocious scene at home when the mother reveals her full animosity toward the child. It is apparent that she thrives on her abuse of the girl.

The sexual problem is dramatized in an account of Maria-Teresa's strange midnight walk with Manuel to a nearby place called the Heritage. Alone with her in the darkness, the boy reveals his strong passion for her. In his frenzy he nearly assaults her—she faints, but soon recovers to find herself unscathed, and the two confused children return to their home. The next day Maria-Teresa returns to the nun's school and finds that as a result of her mother's visit, everyone's manner toward her has changed. For the time being, the incident at the Heritage, if not forgotten, is tucked away in the back of her mind. The narrative moves up to the present, and Maria-Teresa confesses that she has lost her faith. She cannot feel any rapport with the past, with the person she once was: her heart is empty, just as her favorite box and beads have lost their magic fragrance. She has become a different person.

During one of Manuel's frequent illnesses (he has been discovered to be tubercular), Maria-Teresa observes the other side of her mother's nature—the hours of kindness and devotion she shows Manuel. Her mother has become exhausted and haggard but at the same time strangely radiant with happiness and something which must be called love. She seems to be "obsessed by a vision," just as Maria-Teresa was during her fervor to become a nun. But the mother's new love and happiness are not extended to her daughter, and the girl is fearful that Manuel, in his occasional delirium, might reveal the secret of their night visit to the Heritage. In a moment of panic, the girl confesses the whole affair to a priest. Father Garrot displays considerable eagerness to have the whole story, complete with intimate details.

In the portrait of Father Garrot, whose name is significant, we see an appalling misuse of ecclesiastical power. The twisted nature of the man prevents him from observing the secrecy of the confessional, and he shares his special information with Maria-Teresa's mother. Throughout this novel organized religion is portrayed as neurotic, unhealthy, and oppressive. But while the priests, Father Garrot and Father Sanctis, are treated with a devastating irony, the nuns are treated more gently, as sincere but somewhat simple-minded creatures—except the Mother Superior who, for all her machinations, is viewed as essentially a wise woman. This picture is further developed by Manuel, who comes to think of Jesus strictly as a great man and not as God, and by Maria-Teresa who, at communion, feels her sense of religious faith progressively deserting her: some human being is always coming between her and her "vision of heaven." She comes to feel that "true spiritual riches" are for others, not for her.

When Manuel comes to what he calls the "strangest part of my story . . . this interruption of my desire," lasting nearly a month, he sees Maria-Teresa with a "completely disillusioned eye." She seemed to him "nothing but a rather simple-minded child, entirely controlled by her nuns." She would doubtless in time become a religious bigot—one of "those frightful old women one sees at Mass, the last support of a tottering Church." He does not explain this change in attitude toward the girl,

but the implications are that his sexual fixation is merely a
product of an unhealthy mind, one of the evil illusions caused
by bondage to this world, and one which he might transcend
if he could but "distance" himself mentally from the girl, and
associate her with an other evil aspect of this world—the insti-
tution of the Church.

For by now Manuel has nothing but contempt for the Church
and its "black beetles" with their twisted concept of Christ.
Manuel had loved Jesus, in his own way, since childhood, not
as the Christ-God but as "the brave, kind little Man whose
word enchanted men's souls." He believed Christ to be an
understanding friend but in no way supernatural: "In becoming
a Christian I was ceasing to be a Catholic." He thinks of the
absurdity and uselessness of religion in his life, especially in
his present plight—his obsession for the girl and his fear of
death—but he often experiences a "friendly presence" in his
room just before dawn, at which times his loneliness vanishes;
he feels a cool hand on his feverish forehead, "an idea of a
feverish brain which no longer distinguished the possible from
the impossible." With this latter observation the author shows
his usual ambivalence toward "presences"—a phenomenon which
he experienced in his own life but whose nature he does not
attempt to explain. And just as Maria-Teresa had recorded her
negative views of the sinister Father Garrot, so Manuel comments on a young priest with the ironic name of Father Sanctis,
"whose piety, breeding, and good looks drew crowds to his
sermons." But to Manuel "the Latin of Father Sanctis seemed
to bode nothing good, and I have yet to see the priest who did
not carry trouble in the folds of his black gown."

So much for the representatives of the spiritual world. "This
world" is represented in all its material and commercial gross-
ness by Manuel's despicable employer at the bookstore, a tyrannical creature described in terms suitable to a barnyard animal,
and by a M. George Espinchat (a spiney cat?), a smug and
superior clod who comes to stay briefly at Manuel's house.
He is the picture of stupid and insensitive "Success": "Fortune
would smile to the end into that heavy, full-blooded face." He
is the "symbol of the world," and how, Manuel wonders, could
he "contend against such a man and his ilk, those tyrants who
trample on people like me?" So the orthodox religious world,

represented by the priest and nuns, and this world, represented by businessmen, are equally repugnant to Manuel. Both worlds are tyrannical, hypocritical, and vicious; he must create his own world—somewhere "in-between."

A ride to the countryside, to a farmhouse that the family visits on holidays, brings Maria-Teresa's story to a head. The mother is in an unaccountably good humor, and Maria-Teresa feels a pressing need to tell mother all, as she had promised the priest she would do. She feels that time is running out, and her narrative ends with her on the verge of "betraying" Manuel, while he, seeming to sense what she is about to do, never takes his eyes off her.

In an article written shortly after publication of this novel, Green explains how he came to employ his shifting point of view, dropping Maria-Teresa's story and giving the narrative to Manuel. He explains that he chose the first-person narrative because he felt that the effect of truth was heightened by looking through the eyes of Maria-Teresa, "a person too simple to lie and too little the story-teller to exaggerate." But as the story developed, Green suspected that the girl "did not guess with whom she was dealing, and she took for an imbecile a man who was very much her superior." From the moment Green was certain of this, "I abandoned what risked becoming the wrong way, and, without even permitting Maria-Teresa to finish the scene she was telling, I took the words away from her and gave them to Manuel."[5]

And so Part II shifts to Manuel's story, told from his point of view. The narrative now moves gradually and steadily from everyday reality toward total fantasy, and en route we see certain things in a different light than we did in Maria-Teresa's story. But at this moment, Manuel's version picks up at the point where Maria-Teresa's left off, with the dreaded revelation —of the night at the Heritage—about to take place. Manuel, as Maria-Teresa had suspected, is completely aware of what was going on in her mind, and the scene is taut with nervous tension. For one thing, we see Maria-Teresa in a light that would have shocked her. To Manuel, she possesses a beauty of an "indecent quality." She is dressed "in the most provocative manner" by her mother—clothes too tight or too short. This most virtuous mother had made of her daughter "an object of shame and

temptation, something ridiculous and terrible." Yet no one
ever said anything about it, and Maria-Teresa herself seemed
unaware of it. "There again," thinks Manuel, "I was the only one
who saw, the only one who used his eyes." Whether this is an
accurate portrait of Maria-Teresa or merely Manuel's peculiar
reaction to the sexuality of the girl is left to the reader to determine. But it is noteworthy that the young man, who is most
given to fantasy of all the group, considers himself the only
one who sees clearly.

In the ensuing scene, one of the most tense and dramatic in
the book, Manuel is confronted by a cruel dilemma. When,
following Maria-Teresa's confession, he is confronted by the
mother, he denies everything, and the mother then turns on her
daughter, who is hiding under the bed, and heaps venomous
wrath and hatred upon her. For a moment, Manuel is terribly
torn between saving the girl and saving himself, and he is
surprised to find himself quite capable of saying nothing and of
even joining the mother when she forces the girl to beg, on
her knees, for Manuel's forgiveness. He experiences a strange
joy at her submissiveness before him, a mixed sadomasochistic
pleasure as he contemplates her bare legs. Her legs had always
been a source of extreme erotic stimulation to him, and now
he feels "a strange and delicious torment" as he gazes on her.
"There was no question of prayer to banish evil desires; evil
presented itself before me with much too powerful a seduction."
The girls asks for forgiveness, not for having made false accusa-
tions, but for having confessed at all. In a low voice that only
Manuel can hear she apologizes for her "betrayal." Manuel,
overcome by the pressures of the episode, falls ill once again,
and must be helped to bed.

In the past Manuel had exaggerated his illness and had used
it to influence his aunt's feelings toward him, but this time he
is really and seriously sick. He quits his detested job at the
bookstore and spends almost his entire time at home, where he
is free to dream and fill his journal with the products of his
feverish imagination.

During this period, Manuel shows unusual insight into his
aunt's nature. He sees her quite differently than Maria-Teresa
does. He is aware of her complexities and contradictions as
products of, as compensations for, a painful and embittered life.

In her strange kindness and love of invalids he recognizes
the need for power. He also recognizes her willingness, if necessary, to do anything for her daughter Maria-Teresa, whom she
only appears to hate, and he sees the girl's lack of understanding
of her mother's problems. He is also aware that his aunt takes
out her bitterness and admiration toward the man she did not
marry by insulting his son who lacks his father's qualities. For
he has observed that at the peak of one of her vicious verbal
assaults, his aunt will often undergo a paroxysm of emotion,
grasp Manuel to her sobbing bosom, and promise to care for
him always. Nevertheless, his growing loss of religious belief
creates a growing and "necessary" hypocrisy in his relations
with his aunt, who lavishes her love on him in the guise of
"God's love." He feels an increasing contempt for her, as he
continues to nurture evil thoughts regarding her daughter. Maria-
Teresa, oddly enough, displays no hard feelings whatsoever
toward Manuel for his part in the apology scene. She seems to
have forgotten about it, as she conducts herself with what
Manuel considers an almost excessive exuberance and gaiety. He
finds it impossible not to brood about her, especially about her
body—"her great stupid body," her mother would say—and,
thinking of her bare legs, he would be thrown into an emotional
turmoil.

Meanwhile, Manuel has earned for himself a rather bad reputation about the town, mainly because of a game of blindman's
bluff he had played in the woods with a group of girls, friends
of Maria-Teresa, a game which under the guise of innocence
allowed Manuel to grab the girls somewhat more intimately
than some of them thought he ought to. The incident had been
reported to the priests who, true to form, had spread it about
the town. Manuel himself was not ashamed of his actions. He
not only felt no guilt; rather he wished now that he had taken
full advantage of the night at the Heritage. But at the same
time he confesses that he was hopelessly virgin and really afraid
of women: "The idea of Woman aroused a sort of madness in
me and terrified me. By a sort of freak of instinct as strong as
instinct itself, I always tried to shun what I most desired."

Manuel has an overwhelming sense of failure in everything.
But, as usually happens, out of despair rises his concept of Christ,
a sense of a Presence in whom he "believes" in his unorthodox

way. Rejecting the notion of the Saviour, the supernatural Christ of the churches, he turns to "the unknown Christ who was able to stand up to His Family, to the crowd, Himself powerful and great in His humanity . . . His sublime disdain for authority." He makes a strong statement about Christ's virtues as a man, so disguised by the Church who made a god of Him who was the most intrepid of revolutionaries. Manuel grows eloquent on this theme, in a persuasive prose that suggests more of the author than of Manuel. But Manuel's being shunned by the town, along with his reclusive tendencies caused by his recurrent illnesses, results in his turning increasingly to his "childish game"—the "castle game," in which he "beguiles the odious monotony of life by dreaming of *what might have been*" (Manuel's underlining). Reveries become an important part of his notebooks, his "adventures of the mind . . . just as worthy of record as the boring details of a disgusting malady and an unsatisfied passion." Every night, before sleeping, Manuel would take an imaginary walk round the nearby castle. He would "return" with a "strange new story" to be written down the next morning in truthful detail, adding and omitting nothing of the previous evening's imaginative adventure. He describes the nature of his visionary experiences as a state between waking and sleeping, a state when he really *saw*. He admits that, so far, he has never seen the inside of the castle.

In his article on how he wrote *The Dreamer*, Green has given an account of the character and motivations of his young hero, as he saw them:

Actually I wanted to depict a young man inclined towards the meditative life but whose destiny is being falsified by a sudden awakening of the senses. He is not handsome, he is sick, he knows that he is not pleasing, and he is in love. A vain passion; however, all recourses are not closed to him, for the joy that this world refuses him he can come very close to finding in the inner world that he creates in the depths of the night. The dream opens its doors to the "disinherited" and leads him *elsewhere*, into the obscure and marvelous regions where all desires are fulfilled.

But why then, one might ask, did not Manuel, in the freedom of his dreams, create a happy castle, a more joyous experience? Green explains: "But Manuel is as if enchanted by his own sadness [like Green himself?]. Without knowing it, he is a novelist.

He feels, like so many of us, the anguish of living in a world he does not understand, and, in order to escape that anguish, he writes. We create myths to replace an unpleasant reality, but we are not astonished to find in those fables the very fear that we carry within us in ordinary life."[6]

At what point in the story does reality, or Manuel's consciousness of reality, leave off, and total fantasy begin? He seems to relinquish all hold on real life in Chapter 9, when he begins an imaginative life at the castle. He gets a job as "under gardener" and consciously tries to model his life on that of "The Man" and his "disdainful calm before the great ones of the earth." He receives letters from his aunt imploring him to return home—which gives him undisguised pleasure. Throughout these scenes, and during the rest of his stay at the castle, Manuel gives no evidence whatsoever that what he is experiencing is not real. His adventures are described in minute, though almost surrealistic detail, and the reader is persuaded that what he is reading at that time is a realistic account of Manuel's experiences.

Manuel is soon invited into the castle and given the job of reader to a dying old man. In a remote part of the castle, in an airless and silent room, lies the elder member of the Negreterre family, hovering for months between life and death, and it is Manuel's job to read Latin to the invalid for a few hours each day. The Gothic element of the story increases from this point on, and Green exploits one of his favorite themes—the horror of the death room, the terror and fascination of the fatally ill—hovering, clinging to life, sliding from life into death.

The imagery of rooms strikes one as central to this part of the story. The rooms may be enclosed and stuffy, resembling prisons, but even more they represent a kind of security, a womb-like prenatal security. Manuel has succeeded in escaping from the outside world into his own world of disease and death, for each of the inhabitants is concerned with, or related to, some aspect of death. In this connection, we note that Manuel, in his moments of return to the conscious act of writing in his journal, comments on that act as one necessary to fix and retain life, to resist time and annihilation—his journal was born of "fear of ceasing to exist." (Green had begun his own journal in 1928; this novel was published in 1934.) So it appears that Manuel's writings (like Green's) are born both of a desire to escape this world and of a fear of the next world—toward which, however, he is irresistibly drawn.

Both the Vicomtesse of the castle and the head housekeeper, Madame Georges, are embodiments of the imminence of death. Madame Georges, with whom Manuel is obligated to spend considerable time, with her "steadily smiling face," serves as a source of information about what goes on around the castle, and, in an undefined and sinister way, as an agent of death. She is eternally hovering about when death arrives on the scene. Manuel finds the woman repellent but inescapable. From her he learns of the Negreterre family's "traditional way of death." It seems that members of the family all die of the same unnamed disease of which the old man is dying at the moment, and his son Antoine lives in mortal fear of his own eventual demise in the same way. The account of old Monsieur de Negreterre's disease and suffering is pure horror. The old man has an inordinate fear of death, which gives him great strength to linger on, in the most incredible fashion, month after month, in a kind of living death, in virtual solitude, "buried alive." In a sense, he is a man of courage, suffering alone in his airless tomb, interested only in his clock, which is the measure of his victory over death, and he is proud of his resistance to it, even though his pain steadily worsens.

The Vicomtesse is portrayed in a peculiarly ambivalent manner: she is attractive and unattractive; sometimes she seems young and at other times old. She is actually about forty—the same age as Madame Georges, but the Madame is referred to as an old woman, whereas Manuel usually refers to the Vicomtesse as "young." Madame Georges is seen as something alien, as the sinister and brutal aspect of death, whereas Manuel is drawn to the Vicomtesse, who shares his obsession with death and his tendency to have visionary experiences of it. Madame Georges appears as the repellent brute fact; the Vicomtesse, as the imaginative fascination. Manuel discusses his strange visions with her, visions which she also has, and his sense of "presences" of the unseen world hovering about. For, ever since he entered the castle, he has had the sense of being controlled by a will foreign to his own. At times he felt on the verge of confronting "some quite different and much greater Being than ourselves." The Vicomtesse shares this state of mind, though she is often

hysterical, close to derangement. In one dramatic scene, she
calls Manuel to her in the night and tells him of her nocturnal
walk out into the castle grounds, how she felt an unaccountable
happiness as she got farther away from Negreterre—away from
death. She had found a "sanctuary" from death in the "protecting depths of the night." But she had to return on hearing, or
thinking she heard, her father cry out. She launches into a
diatribe against Madame Georges—her hatred and fear of the
repellent woman, who has "the superhuman stupidity of Death,"
who is perhaps "Death itself."

Manuel is horrified as the Vicomtesse describes Madame
Georges's grip on the Negreterre household, her dominance
over all its aspects, her ability to implicate herself insidiously
in family affairs. "She attracts irresistibly to herself those who
fear her most, first my brother, then myself." They could no
no longer get rid of the hateful woman. "When my father dies
she will go and install herself by someone else's bedside." Madame
Georges is, in her way, in love with the Negreterre castle and is
extremely possessive toward it, whereas the Negreterre family
would like nothing better than to escape from it. Yet they—
the Vicomtesse and Antoine—are always drawn back—by "curiosity," says the Vicomtesse, by which she means a morbid attraction to disease and death and a desire to know "how life ends."
Manuel also hates Negreterre, but he too is unable to leave:
some strange "bond" holds him in the house. The Vicomtesse
is obsessed with her father's illness and gives her own imaginative version of what her father is experiencing, his sense of moving between two worlds, and gives her "reading" of what dead
people "see and know," which she gathered from studying the
face of a dead sister. "Life is an illusion . . . the only reality is
death." And she says that she has heard her dying father mutter
the secret of the dead: "the world which we think we see does
not exist." This world is a mere illusion shattered by the advent
of death, the only reality. The point is made that such deep
thoughts can cause one to lose the world, which then must be
"reconstructed" by effort of the will.

These necrophiliac conversations are ended brutally on the
occasion of a nocturnal visit by Manuel to the Vicomtesse's
room. It happens that on the very night the old man dies, Manuel
and the Vicomtesse, drawn together by mutual obsessions, engage

in a bizarre sexual act. Afterward, Manual finds himself unable
to extricate himself from her frenzied and all-enveloping embrace.
They fall together to the floor, where he finally manages to
disengage her clinging arms. But when he looks at the Vicomtesse, she appears strangely altered. Her flesh is cold. She is
dead.

Manuel makes his escape through the confusion of a great
crowd of people on the staircase. He runs out of the castle and
into the park. He thinks he hears a voice calling after him, but
he does not turn around. He runs through the park gates feeling
a heavy grip on his heart, aware of the looming of the silent and
forbidding castle which had "sheltered my sadness." He leaves
the castle grounds "with regret."

In Part III, "Maria-Teresa's story (concluded)," we observe
Manuel at work writing incessantly in his journal. He is totally
involved; he neither hears nor replies to questions from Maria-
Teresa. He never leaves the house because, as his aunt says, the
town is full of enemies. She frequently gives vent to her hostility to the townsfolk, especially the priests and Manuel's
father confessor in particular. Manuel continually suffers from
the heat, which is transferred to his adventures at the castle—
throughout his narrative of the castle he suffered from the heat.
His illness and continual coughing, says Maria-Teresa, "gradually
became a part of our daily life." But Manuel shunned doctors—
he sought only his aunt's solace and attention. Her devotion
to him is unflagging: she never scolds, and she is always dressed
up attractively for him—though she claims it is only because
someone from the archbishopric might unexpectedly call. Maria-
Teresa is also obliged to be constantly well dressed, but she is
soon sent away to boarding school, and she can record only what
she observes on her return during Christmas vacation.

Maria-Teresa notices that on her return from school she is
treated to a cool reception by both her mother and Manuel.
Her presence is obviously a nuisance, an "interruption" of their
family life which she no longer shares. But she now feels quite
grown up and no longer fears her mother. She pressures Manuel
into going for a walk to the castle, something he agrees to with
great reluctance. He obeys, almost mechanically, obviously terribly shaken by the whole idea. Their walk develops into a devastating experience: the castle turns out to be nothing but an old

farmhouse which had been changed into a castle in their child-ish minds. "Of the picture I had created of it in my mind, nothing remained. I had seen the castle only through Manuel's eyes until this day." Manuel walks on as if in a trance and collapses in the woods. As he lies with his head in Maria-Teresa's lap, he unex-pectedly avows his love for her, then dies muttering something about "It's nearly happiness."

The narrative shifts to some years later. The mother is utterly changed by illness and sorrow resulting from Manuel's death, but Maria-Teresa has little pity for her. The girl, now a young woman, discover's Manuel's journals and spends hours reading his vivid and immensely detailed story. She finds herself reliving her childhood (which is reflected in her own recorded story) and is impressed by the overwhelming realism of Manuel's tale of life at the castle. She knows that the story is not based on "even the shadow of fact," that Manuel never left the house. She feels overwhelmingly sad: "The whole street seemed haunted, and the steps of a passerby who hugged the white wall opposite echoed in my ears with a muffled far-away sound, as in a dream." We recall, at this point, that Manuel, when working at his jour-nal, spent hours of each day staring at the white wall of the prefecture across the street. Its blank surface had been a recur-rent image, strongly suggesting a parallel with the Vicomtesse's insistence that life is nothingness, that beyond the hills, beyond the wall of falling rain, there is nothing. All is illusion.

And yet, Maria-Teresa muses, making a point that carries much of the meaning of the book: "As I shut the last of these little books I asked myself whether the Dreamer, after all, does not cast a keener eye on this world than we do, and whether, in a world which is surrounded by the invisible, the illusions of desire and of death are not just as real as our delusive reality."

II Midnight

Like many of Green's novels, *Midnight* (*Minuit*, 1936)[7] begins with what appears to be conventional realism but soon moves toward fantasy. A lonely carriage is traveling slowly over empty, windswept fields. In contrast to the silence and emptiness are the violence and hostility that arises from the carriage, as the occu-pants hurl threats and curses at the driver. The carriage stops.

A woman gets out and walks along to the side of a hill where, watching a train go by, she takes out a knife and kills herself. There is not a word of explanation, only description. The narrative then turns to the brutality and loneliness of the orphan's world—the child Elizabeth among her harsh and neurotic aunts. She learns of her mother's death, spends most of a terrifying night in an aunt's gloomy house, and flees into the darkness. After running away, she spends a frightening night in town, hiding in the shadows. She is discovered by a warmhearted stranger who takes her home to become, for a number of years, a member of his family. We then see her as a teen-ager with a growing intrest in the opposite sex. As in the case of Adrienne Mesurat and her doctor, Elizabeth focuses her attention on a handsome knife grinder, whose regular passing by the house she eagerly awaits. But unlike Adrienne's doctor, the knife grinder is aware of the girl's interest, and, in a dreamlike episode, she follows him, losing herself for a time in the maze of the town.

A Monsieur Agnel arrives on the scene, bringing a message from an unknown relative who claims Elizabeth and takes her to live, for no accountable reason, in a great dark mansion, Font-froide, where she is kept a virtual prisoner. The huge, mysterious house is apparently full of inhabitants, but the inmates remain largely unseen, especially the master, Monsieur Edme, who seems to keep entirely to his room. The strange and vaguely sinister Monsieur Agnel looks after Elizabeth, seeing to it that she does not wander off. She forms an odd relationship with another young lady inmate of the mansion and develops a passion for a young manservant, Serge. She discovers that Monsieur Edme is her mother's former lover, the man who deserted her mother and was the cause of her suicide while she watched the departing train carrying him away. She also learns that Monsieur Edme has gathered a bizarre collection of people in his house for the purpose of holding midnight ceremonies, mysterious séances consisting primarily of impassioned harangues by Monsieur Edme on the superiority of the visionary life, a life of the imagination, possible only in the darkness of night, when one can transcend the limitations of physical existence and move into an ideal world of one's own creation.

As Monsieur Edme represents the appeal of the nocturnal supersensual realm of midnight, so Serge represents, for Elizabeth, the sensual physical world of everyday. She plans to escape with Serge, but she is temporarily captivated by Monsieur Edme's hypnotic appeal, as she hides in an anteroom and witnesses the strange nocturnal gathering to which she has not been invited. Serge gets her away from Monsieur Edme's influence by hiding with her in an upstairs room, where the young pair, while waiting an opportunity to escape the mansion, engage in a sexual act, which Elizabeth finds to be a most painful affair. Serge, when about to be apprehended by Monsieur Edme and Agnel, shoots at Monsieur Edme but kills Agnel, who dies protecting his master. Serge, trying to escape through a window, falls to his death, and Elizabeth, in a frenzy of despair, follows him in a suicide leap.

In the closing paragraph, as Elizabeth dies, she sees a vision of the old servant Agnel coming toward her, his face illuminated by radiant happiness and infinite kindness (we are reminded at this point that his name suggests a combination of *agneau* [lamb] and angel). This image of humble devotion and service lifts Elizabeth and carries her upward and away from the earth by what she feels to be "an irresistible force."

Midnight has been aptly described as a "psychic" novel. Common logic of cause and effect holds no authority in this story in which the action is governed by unpredictable tangents of forces unnamed, unseen, unlimited by earthly laws. The characters are psychological counterparts of their backgrounds, distorted puppets that dance on strings leading to no traceable source. They are shadow actors outside time and space. Here Green is the master of what Gabriel Marcel has called "*la technique de l'inconfort.*"[8] That is, Green refuses to grant the usual mental satisfaction of traditional literature. He is a writer by inner necessity; he writes as he must; and therefore he is indifferent to the reactions and demands of his readers. He leads us into an incomprehensible world and shows us characters performing grotesque actions and making fantastic speeches. What, indeed, are we to make of Monsieur Edme's harangue—that mysterious character who appears only at the end of the novel but who was in command throughout? He is the "magician-king" of his strange domain; apparently, he is also a sort of pastor overseeing his flock of lost souls—hoping to lead them into the promised land beyond. Green says, in his

Journal, that Monsieur Edme is one "who seeks to impose his will on the inhabitants of Fontfroide, and Fontfroide, the great mansion, is here like the image of his entire personality. Monsieur Edme represents reason as it is continually solicited by the dream."

After the suicide of his mistress, Monsieur Edme had bought a huge isolated mansion, formerly inhabited by nuns: Fontfroide. He had tried to poison himself but had survived and has gathered around him an assemblage of bizarre beings, lost souls, some mad or nearly so, others gnawed by an internal acid, a spiritual poison; and he has taught them all the essential truth that night is superior to day and that by starlight the most banal life becomes an adventure. He preaches that, liberated from the gross illusions of day, the soul aspires only to the realm of the invisible, and it remembers what it thought it had never known. When the body acts in broad daylight, it remains plunged in a protective torpor; but at midnight it awakens gently, happily, in its great nocturnal paradise. Monsieur Edme tends to see the "real" Fontfroide in a recurrent dream which he describes, in impassioned terms, to his entranced listeners—a mansion which "shines gently in the dream like a castle of glass enveloped in mist." There, in this visionary mansion, is

the real refuge against the terrors of this life, the fortress of the soul into which no hatred can enter, where fear is dissipated and in which the mind casts off its exhausting burden of lies and illusions. Seen from there, our own world appears in a dim, cold, dreary light like that of the first streaks of dawn. We wake out of an evil dream. Death, sickness, the disappointments of love, ruin are all a nightmare; and everything which is real is in this other world. . . . There no storms threaten a peacefulness that will never end. A perpetual transparent, luminous night bathes its quite spacious rooms with its rays. Through the uncurtained windows one can see a sheet of white mist which swirls along close to the ground between the black poplars, and in the sky, in the depths of a blue darkness which is never troubled by the glare of the sun, one can see the stars. The mind travels from abyss to abyss between the worlds. A strange ecstasy upsets all our thoughts, a strange happiness, my friends, something like a long spell of giddiness without the terror of falling, and a feeling of infinite liberty. From that ethereal dwelling to which I want to take you the soul can issue with the same ease with which

we leave our Fontfroide here. If you cast off the terrible burden
which we have to bear from birth to death, you will soar, as I do,
to the eternally calm regions of supernatural happiness.

But what is this visionary world? In what sense does it
possess "reality"? In his depiction of the inmates of Fontfroide,
Green gives us a spectacle of desolation, of "larval" existences
dragging themselves toward ruin and death; yet he imposes on
them a curious mysterious benediction. The heroine Elizabeth
arrives at Fontfroide only after having experienced the "real
world"—she has been terrorized by some people and wel-
comed and cherished by others—and she has felt the frantic
impulses of the flesh without having the total experience. Is
there a correspondence relating the inhabitants of Fontfroide
to all the people she has known, each of which had made an
imprint on her? Is Serge the counterpart of the knife grinder?
We cannot be certain. It is clear, however, that we are in the
presence of a work in which everything is symbolic, none of
whose symbols can be made entirely precise. One is sure that
Green himself does not have the key. Hence the *"technique
de l'inconfort."* Is Monsieur Edme a deceived illusionist, a
poor lunatic, or is he in possession of a second reality not
given to others to see? It is impossible to say. At times Green
seems on the verge of revelation, but he never makes it. His
world is "suspended between an all too real Hell and a Heaven
provided only by miraculous moments of vision." The suspense
appears to be part of a game, some mental acrobatics, but it is
actually the result of an inner pressure of necessity, which
governs all that Green writes.[9]

In *Midnight* the perorations of Monsieur Edme appear to
support the judgment expressed by Maria-Teresa at the end
of *The Dreamer*, when she suggests that the *"Visionnaire"*
sees more clearly than the rest of us and that, "in a world
surrounded by the invisible, the illusions of desire" are "just
as real as our delusive reality." So we are confronted by a
choice of illusions: since everything in this life is illusory, why
not give our credence to visions that appear to transcend the
limits of the visible? But the trouble with this is that, throughout Green's fiction, from Daniel O'Donovan to Monsieur Edme,
the visions of "higher illusions" are products of feverish and
unhealthy minds, and unless we are to posit some post-

Romantic view that disease is akin to genius and is a valid means
of penetrating into "ultimate reality," we are forced to the
conclusion that such visions are but examples of wishful
thinking and are in no way superior to the ordinary illusions of
this world. But, as Green would say, one writes as one must. And,
continuing to write from inner compulsion, he ventured even
further into the realm of the fantastic in his next two novels.

III   Then Shall the Dust Return *and* If I Were You

In *Then Shall the Dust Return* (*Varouna*, 1940, 1941),[10]
Green's preoccupation with the realm of night moves from
the scenic and dramatic to the philosophic. Night becomes
more than the setting and occasion for miraculous happen-
ings; it becomes identified with the supreme deity which presides
over the destinies of men, in the form of "Varouna," the Vedic
god of nocturnal sky, who oversees the lives of the guilty of this
world.[11] In giving this name to his novel, Green explains that,
under the laws of Varouna, a "crime committed in one life
will be expiated only in another life, centuries later, but I don't
want it to be a story of reincarnation"[12]—though that, in fact, is
what the novel appears to be about. During the 1930's Green
had been reading deeply into philosophic works, especially
those of the East, and these form much of the substance of
Varouna and its companion piece, *If I Were You*. In the first
work, the action extends over a thousand-year period and
shows us two beings inescapably attracted to each other who
rediscover and love each other in various lives down through
the centuries. The two people live through a series of reincarnations—as Hoël, Bertrand Lombard, and the novelist Jeanne
—having their love frustrated during their early existences and,
on one occasion, even killing each other, and finally achieving
unity in their last incarnation. It is a strange story, suggesting
that the individual soul is not bounded by time and space and
that it might require a succession of lives for individual destinies
to be realized. "These avatars of a couple," Green says,
"described in *Varouna*, are transformed in *If I Were You* in a
continual substitution of one person for another, in the same
individual." The two novels are therefore related and share
the illuminations brought to their author by his studying of

the *Baghavad Gita*, the *Ramakrishna*, Myers' *Human Personality and Its Survival of Bodily Death*, Moukergi's *Le Visage du Silence*, and the works of Rudolf Steiner.[13]

But is metempsychosis or the transmigration of souls the subject of *Varouna*? What the author apparently wanted to do was simply to show that a single existence scarcely represents more than an unintelligible fragment in the long obscure "message" created by a series of generations. That is, one generation, one life, is not sufficient for the working out of individual destinies. So, from generation to generation runs a chain of being, like that real chain of metal which, in the story, is cast up on the beach, at the feet of Hoël, by a great ocean wave. After the misadventures of Hoël, the first in the series of avatars, and his mistress, the story leaps ahead several centuries, into the second episode during the French Renaissance. Here the chain reappears as Helène Lombard relates the life of her father Bertrand Lombard and explains to us how the chain is passed from hand to hand. The chain crops up again, four centuries later, in the final tableau, which takes place between 1905 and 1914. Here Jeanne, a novelist, diligently keeps her daily journal, a document which bears a strong resemblance to the notebooks of Green, and reveals that Green has been traveling the realms of Eastern thought only to find himself back at the door of the Catholic Church. He explains: "The development which was to bring me to the Church, beginning in 1938, had begun in 1935, that is to say, well in advance of *Varouna*. Whence the nature of several scenes: Hoël, at the moment of being hanged, understands that the Father opens his arms to him [as did Elizabeth, in *Midnight*, at the moment of her death]; a person invites the bystanders to recite the Lord's Prayer; and finally, there is that tiny cross passed to the neck of Jeanne with the exorcised chain at the end of the book."[14]

These evidences of Christian faith, of Green's return to the Church, are much less explicit in the companion novel, *If I Were You* (*Si j'étais vous*, 1947, 1949).[15] It was during his stay at the University of Virginia that Green got the idea of telling the story of a man who, after having made a bargain with the devil, obtains the power to change bodies with any person of his choice, merely by pronouncing some magic words.

The story was to be called *Baphomet,* the name the Templars gave to the prince of this world, Lucifer. This manuscript of 1922 was set aside until 1944 when it was taken up and made into the fantastic tale we now have. He worked on it for three years, until 1947, when it appeared under the present title.[16]

Green tells his readers, in the foreword, that the book is "an attempt to set out in order certain matters which have puzzled me ever since I was a child." It is the question of identity: why one was one's self and not somebody else, and what it would be like to be another person. There are only two kinds of men who succeed in escaping from the prison of their own bodies, Green tells us: poets (including novelists) and mystics: "No small portion of our innate discontent arises from the perpetual sameness in which we are enveloped; from the fact that we are faced every morning as we awake with the problem of finding a solution to the same ever-recurring question, which is how we are to keep ourselves going till nightfall, or indeed till death." In telling this story, Green tried to avoid any "philosophical bias"; rather, he has tried to make of it, "for all its inherent fantasy, a precisely detailed account of events taking place in a town in the north of France in the year 1920, or thereabouts."

It is a story of a young man, Fabian, who, hating his personal ugliness and poor health, desires to become someone else. His wish is granted by a mysterious stranger who takes him in a closed carriage on a nocturnal visit to a distant mansion, where he is given a magic formula enabling him to change bodies and minds with other persons, while yet retaining a vestige of his original intellect, along with the memory of the formula, in order that he may return, when he wishes, to his original self. He works through a series of metamorphoses, all of them unpleasant: his aged but wealthy employer, a robust young ruffian who turns to murder, a sexually repressed bookworm, and a handsome young man married to a beautiful but, as it turns out, cold and designing woman. This young man, Fabian's last "avatar," is the object of adoration by a lovely cousin Elise, from whose point of view one section of the story is told. The unhappy husband (now inhabited by Fabian) sets things somewhat straight by punishing his wife (long overdue) for her malicious selfishness and by telling Elise straight out of the impossibility of her dreams and desires, so that she might be free to find another life of her own. The point of view then shifts back to Fabian as he leaves the great house to seek his first self, whom he eventually finds after long searching. He finds his original person dying, but he manages nonetheless to change places. He is ready to accept death in his original form, having discovered the impossibility of achieving happiness, by metamorphosis or other means, in this world, where everyone has his share of pain and suffering. The only exception to the pattern was a little boy, whose body and soul Fabian desired to inhabit. But this time the formula failed: against the innocence of a child in a state of grace the sorcery of the dark powers could not prevail.

It has been suggested that the key to the novel is given by a line from Green's *Journal*: "It must be shown that this desire for necessary transformations corresponds to the desire not to die."[17] Green develops this idea at the end of his foreword to the novel: "And were I called upon to sum up concisely the content of the book I would perhaps say that it deals with a certain anguish of mind, that double anguish that consists in the knowledge that a man can escape neither his own destiny nor the approach of death and the bewilderment of finding himself alone in the midst of an incomprehensible universe."

Almost all of Green's characters, as we have seen, are, at one time or another, struck by a sense of the nothingness of this world. "I am not living—I am dreaming that I am living. Or better, I am dreaming that I am living while knowing that the dream is not true." Behind all that surrounds us, there is nothing. Real life lies elsewhere. This theme echoes throughout the novels. Man lives in a deceptive and deceitful world— matter is but a façade, an imposture. As a result, the author's concern with the details of the real world is frequently interrupted by description of a character's dreams. Similarly, certain settings acquire reality for the author only when they have been "improved" by the fantastic; thus his descriptions of the real tend to become surreal. Nature offers us, in certain places and times, kinds of transitional experiences between the real and unreal zones of half-color, such as that sought by the protagonist of *L'Autre Sommeil*, the most personal of Green's books: "I have a very special affection for the places where life

appears under an unreal aspect.... Two steps farther on, a
place resumes the form we know all too well, but there, at that
specially elected point, it has something of the uncertain about
it which relates it to dream." Such places, as we have seen,
include certain old houses, unfinished structures, edges of
cemeteries, quais of the Seine, coal or lumber yards. The
preferred times are nightfall, midnight, and just before dawn.
Nighttime affords passage from the known to the unknown:
"The night, the night—of all times I have felt that it was
the most favorable to me." Night means for Green "the fading
away of the world of appearances, of the world lit up by the
sun, with its colors and its perpetual noise of speech. It accom-
plishes in the domain of the senses what we would like
to be able to accomplish in the domain of the spirit, and what
it proposes to our eyes of flesh inevitably attracts the inner
vision. Before this vision, everything that arises from our
daily life becomes insignificant. Our individual fate and the
fate of nations are brought back into their true proportions,
that is to say, to zero."[18] He says in *To Leave Before Dawn,*
"I am writing this towards the end of the afternoon. It is a
good time to look over one's shoulder and look back at the
day, before the coming of night, because the night is another
world. When the light has faded, the stars will shine. Then
the black sky will say what it has to say."

According to some critics, the sun is usually the synonym
for unhappiness in Green's works: "Tragedy arrives on sunny
days." Green says the same thing in his *Journal,* but the novels
do not consistently support him in this. And in one of his most
recent books he states that "at the age of six or more, I had
a horror of darkness that cannot be described. If I have ever
known fear, it certainly originated there."[19] Night and its
shadows terrify children and adults alike. Menace lurks in
dark closets, and footsteps are heard mounting the dark
stairways. Adrienne Mesurat is terrified at night (she quotes
Racine: *"C'était pendant l'horreur d'une profonde nuit"*), and
it is in the darkness that she pushes her father to his death down
the staircase. She finds nothing but horror and nightmare in
the strange hotel rooms. Both *The Dark Journey* and *The
Strange River* are nocturnal novels. Guéret in *Dark Journey*
scales a wall at night to enter Angèle's room, only to find her

gone; and later, after leaving her for dead (the murderous act *is* committed in broad daylight), he prowls about in the dark and spends a weird night in a coalyard, with only rats for company. Philip, in *The Strange River*, wanders around at night, and he is attracted to the somber darkness of the river Seine, where he witnesses a fatal fight between a man and a woman on the quai. He fails to intervene, though he knows he should, because he fears the darkness of the quai and the black, silently running river, which both fascinates and repels him. That failure, in the darkness, will change his life. Similarly, Wilfred, in *Each Man in His Darkness*, is a nocturnal creature, prowling about in low dives in search of available women. The night and its darkness are of course metaphorical, representing a spiritual and moral darkness—souls are lost in the eternal night. On occasion, when certain characters lift their eyes to the starry heavens, they feel transported out of this dark world of misery. But many of the characters never lift their eyes. They remain in the dark, full of fear. And some, to be sure, do prefer the night. Monsieur Edme and his "guests," in *Midnight*, organize their lives around the night: midnight is the most favorable time for spiritual meditation and transfiguration.

So darkness and night in Green's novels seem to be ambivalent, conducive to evil as well as being an escape and refuge from evil. After all, "each man is in his darkness," seeking the light—at least that is what these novels say. In his *Journal,* Green gives us a somewhat different attitude toward night: "The sky was a dark blue and the stars spoke that language that words cannot render, but which will always trouble me, because it is addressed to what is most true in us. I lose myself in contemplation of nocturnal sky just as others throw themselves from a bridge to put an end to things, but for me, it is to find again what I have sought since my childhood, and when I gaze at the stars, I cannot be entirely unhappy."[20] "Such a spectacle," Green tells us, "annihilates the human language. Even the effect it produces in us lies beyond words. A great happiness, a deep feeling of the vanity of the world, a more mysterious feeling which is analogous to that of the presence of God, an enormous silence within us, which is like an echo of the silence of the heavens."[21] The experienced emotion is so strong that, beyond a certain intensity, it can find in words only a pale equivalence, and the nocturnal stroller, who returns from the avenues of the night where, in a prodigious moment, he felt God, can scarcely communicate his experience.

By night Green means, not the dark and shadowy byways of this world, but the spacious heavens, illumined with bright stars. That is his concept of night—upward-looking. The description of Fabian, in *If I Were You*, is probably Green's most eloquent statement of his experiences with the starry night. Fabian is gazing out of his window:

Above the roofs in the vast recesses of the black sky myriads of stars were twinkling. . . . Whenever he stared like this into the all-enveloping night he had a sensation of being lifted gently above the world. There was something about those glittering pin points of light arranged in a secret pattern which fascinated him like a riddle the meaning of which he could not interpret and which at times irritated and at other times soothed his inmost spirit. As the minutes passed, the longer he looked the more he had the sensation of being raised above the window and the house itself, although he was all the while conscious of the solid ledge upon which his arms were resting. It was almost as if by the very effort of gazing into space a sort of gulf in himself, corresponding to the giddy depths into which his imagination peered, was being opened. Nothing on this earth, he thought—if indeed it was as microscopic a fragment in the universe as astronomers averred—could be of any real importance. And yet, however inconsiderable it might be, and however insignificant the creature who inhabited it, each one had none the less this infinity of stars within him. And shutting his eyes Fabian contemplated for a moment that strange world made up of numberless lights until, lost like a child in a dark room, panic-stricken, he reopened his eyes quickly and gazed once more into the void which yet rocked about him under the influence of a nameless terror. At the same time the conviction came over him that a whole part of himself was being drawn out of him through his eyes, and that the boldest and truest part.

Green continues, in words that closely parallel experiences related in his journals:

It is to be understood that nothing of all this formulated itself into any definite mold in his [Fabian's] mind; and yet at the same time nothing could have seemed so intensely real. Ever since childhood he had been haunted by a feeling of some inner presence which, in some way that he could not have described, was ever beyond the

reach of his own consciousness and yet was set free the moment he
raised his eyes to the night sky. It was impossible to put this feeling
into words, as it was equally impossible for Fabian to find words
to describe so many of the loveliest things of this world. . . . No one
could hope to do more than compass vague allusions to such things
which it remained for each one to interpret after his own fashion.
And thus it was that in the face of the tender light of the stars
above him Fabian experienced all the bitterness of a dumb man
trying desperately to give expression to what is in him, and he
wondered whether in fact man had ever been capable of delivering
his soul of the weight imposed upon it by those same stars.

And the unhappy Guéret, in *The Dark Journey,* looks out
of the window which his drab and unloved wife has just
thrown open: "The sky suddenly appeared as part of the
room, filling it with its stars and shadows. In spite of his
melancholy the man turned his head and looked at it; all at
once something made his heart beat quicker, a confused
yearning toward that silent immensity which seemed to beckon
to him. What peace lay in the depths of that black sky after
the babble of human speech! 'Oh, to be happy!' . . . One by one
the shutters closed in upon the room."

But, as frequent notations in the *Journal* make clear, the
depths of the sky do not, for Green, always afford a sense of
peace. Lying outside time and space, they remind one of his
own temporal and physical limitations; they remind one of
death. Once, when very young, and observing the stars, Green
had, "like some sort of revelation, the feeling of the immense
sadness of the universe. . . . I experienced for the first time a
melancholy that I have never been able to drive entirely from
my mind." Another time he records: "Since my fifteenth year
I have always lived with the feeling of danger which almost
never ceases. I say almost." In fact, the only time Green was
really happy was during his early years when writing his
"inexplicably somber" novels—then he was so happy that sometimes he could not sleep for pure joy of being alive. These brief
periods of happiness are spots of bright color in a life that
tended toward the gray of melancholy. Why? He often asks
himself: "It is the sadness of belonging to this world. I cannot
be completely happy in a world where death always has the
last word and where it can intervene at any moment." Death,

for Green, is ever present. "Death sits at the table with us. It slides into our beds, we sleep with it, but it sleeps with only one eye closed. At the least touch of illness, it whispers in our ear: 'Don't forget me, eh? I will be back.'"

Darkness, despair, and anguish are related to the general menace of fatality, outside human range or grasp, yet precisely designated. It is the anguish of the human condition, of being tied to a body and to an earth under domination of time and death: "That menace, what is it if not the menace of death which weighs on us, no matter what our age?" For the passing of time is a principal source of malaise: "Anyone who has not awakened just before dawn and felt the anguish of passing life —that person will not like my book." The novels and journals abound in references to fear of death—a pall cast over all life because everything must end: annihilation awaits everything; every sunset is a small death. The novels dramatize the problem, but the *Journal* is the actual means of combating time and death: "To let a detail escape is to let escape a little of life itself, for our past life has no other reality than in our memory and it must be able to retain it entirely until death." The *Journal* is the expression of "the eternal desire to capture the passing instant in words," but all such attempts to retain the past are futile. In spite of everything, "one has the impression of not having existed . . . everything precipitates itself toward nothingness with an irresistible force." Still, one writes—the novels and journals are a response to the world of night and death; they are, as one critic has expressed it, "prayers against time."

CHAPTER 5

Autobiography and Art

I The "Impossible Love"

G REEN'S early preoccupation with purity and the problem of nudity carried over into his mature years and figures prominently in his last two novels. In the autobiographical *Terre Lointaine* (1966), he discusses his experiences as a student at the University of Virginia, and we find that the problems which afflicted him as a child of six had remained unchanged, both as regards the form they took and his difficulty in understanding them. He recalls, for example, that in the vestibule of one of the buildings at the university there were two statues, Myron's *Discus Thrower* and the *Hermes of Praxiteles* carrying a Bacchus on his arm, "proud and nobly voluptuous." "I always experienced a vague disquietude in turning my gaze toward that young man whose nudity seemed, in an indefinable manner, much more complaisant than that of the discus thrower. It troubled me to see those statues, especially when in the presence of other students, and I entered the class rooms with a feeling of uneasiness that did not leave me."[1] Later he describes how, on passing the statues, he would always lower his eyes, trying not to look, but "not to look was for me an ordeal just as looking was another, and I would find it difficult to say which made me suffer the most. Once again, as when I was six years old viewing 'The Bearers of Bad News,' I felt myself the prey of desires about which I understood nothing."[2]

His situation was brought home to him, clearly and forcibly, on the occasion of a lecture given by one of his professors on the subject of some lines from Virgil. The professor, saying it was useless to disguise the meaning of the passage under consideration, explained that it was an example of "the shame of antiquity, the love of boys." Green recalls:

111

These words fell in a prodigious silence. . . . The extreme attention
with which these words were heard should have taught me something, if I had been capable of reasoning, but I sat there as dumbfounded as if I had received a blow on the head. In the space of
a second I understood a thousand things, except one which was
essential. I understood that the strange passion of which Virgil was
speaking was also in me. A flash of light illuminated my whole life.
I was frightened by that revelation that showed me to be similar
to the youths of antiquity. The shame of antiquity, I carried it in
myself. I carried it in myself alone. Between generations vanished
for more than twenty centuries and myself, there existed this extraordinary bond. In the modern world I was alone because of it. It
was as if, to the original sin from which we all suffer, there had
been added another which reached nobody but me, for the im-
probable thing about this whole story was that I believed myself
alone in experiencing that disquieting love. "The shame of antiquity . . ." If he had said, "The shame of all times," my reaction
might have been quite different, but as I viewed the matter, my
place was in the world before Christ.

He closed his Virgil with a strange feeling, a mixture of horror
and a "vague and cruel satisfaction." " 'In any case, *they* would
have understood me.' Not to be understood by any but the
dead, the dead fallen into dust . . . that was something to darken
my thoughts."[3]
    Green stresses throughout *Terre Lointaine* that his relations
with the young men to whom he was powerfully attracted at
that time remained pure of all carnality. "The desire which
seized my entrails on viewing the blind Hermes, that desire was
never connected with love such as I conceived it. The two, it
seemed to me, were essentially different. Because of that, I
never dreamed of reproaching myself in confessing to that violent
and total love. The poets often spoke of their flames. The flame in
me was truly a devouring fire that burned up every carnal
thought before it would even approach my heart."[4] This sense of
a devouring fire is echoed in Green's epigraph to *Julien Green par
lui-même*: "*Je sais ce que c'est que le feu. Le feu est ma patrie.*"
    These passages have been quoted at length because, when we
consider certain novels, especially *L'Autre Sommeil* (*The Other
Sleep*), *The Transgressor*, *Moira*, *Each in His Darkness*, and
the play *South* (*Sud*), we find that these passages cast consid-

erable light on comparable episodes in Green's works of fiction
and drama.

Two of Green's novels take the form, in a sense, of a diptych,
with each panel showing the opposite aspect of the problem of
sexuality. *Moira* (1950, translated in 1951) depicts the fate of a
country boy who comes to the large and sophisticated university
bringing with him a fanatical puritanism and an incredible ignorance of the fleshly world. The other side of the diptych is given by
Each in his Darkness (1961), which portrays the moral con-
vulsions of a young man who is attractive, charming in the eyes
of women, and a dedicated lecher. Both young men come to a
bad end, but to each is held out the possibility of salvation.

While each of these novels includes characters who are victims of the "impossible love," the protagonists are essentially
heterosexual, and their amorous lives are directly related to the
larger problem of religious faith. The theme of homosexual
love is central, however, to *L'Autre Sommeil, The Transgressor,*
and *Sud.* The theme made its first explicit appearance in *L'Autre
Sommeil,* which was written in 1931 but never translated.[5] In
this story the young Denis experiences a strong physical attraction to first his cousin Claude and then to another boy. A brief
affair with a girl, Andrée, does nothing to alleviate his chaste but
ardent passion for Claude, a passion whose nature Claude does
not grasp. As in all Green's portrayals of such passions, Denis
seeks to enlighten his cousin, but in vain. He is not understood.
The main theme of the story centers around Denis' stubborn
resistance to the strange seductiveness which the two other
youths exert upon him, but this resistance is complicated by
Denis' divided nature; for struggling for ascendancy within him
are the opposite feelings of the joy of life and its terrible
burdens: specifically, the sufferings caused by his self-imposed
sensual privation and, at the same time, his feeling certain that
he is destined for a life of pleasure. His capacity for love, however, is focused entirely on the other two youths. His father inspires him only with fear and disgust, and with the death of the
old man, the boy feels only a sense of deliverance. Similarly,
he has no love for his mother; he merely enjoys watching her,
in the odd belief that he resembles her. During the night of her
death, he spends his time reading *Manon Lescaut,* for, to Denis,
to become an orphan means only to break chains. And, to further

underline his sense of revolt, he refers to Catholicism as "superstition" and claims that he is not a Christian (the story was written during Green's estrangement from the Church). Throughout the story we feel that we are on the threshold of something that is obscure and terrible but never formulated. Tensions are resolved only by the abrupt revelations of a death. The story remains continually on the verge of the fantastic without ever actually crossing the line. Its subject is more fully developed in subsequent works, especially in *Sud* and *The Transgressor*.

II   The Transgressor

The Transgressor (*Le Malfaiteur*, 1956)[6] has much of interest, stemming largely from its theme, but it cannot be considered one of Green's more successful works. It is excellently written and contains some striking portraits, but its various themes and passages are not adequately fused into a satisfying whole. The story operates on two levels and is written in two styles. The major theme—an unusual love triangle between a woman and two men—is portrayed in a tone of solemn intensity; the second theme—the plight of the downtrodden in a world dominated by the insensitive bourgeoisie—is presented in a satiric manner which at times turns into grotesque comedy. As in the earlier *The Strange River*, the personal conflicts and tragedies of the protagonists are played out against a background of social criticism. In the earlier work the personal problems of the main character are an aspect and a product of the bourgeois world of which he is the living emblem. Flaws of character and flaws of the social order are one and the same. But in *The Transgressor* the relationship is not established. A part of the novel is devoted to the tragicomic life of poor Félice, the humble seamstress, and her relations with her overbearing employers and with her constant companion, the humanized mannequin named Blanchonnet who dominates that part of her life and dreams which are not dominated by her masters. And her masters, the upperclass residents of the great mansion, are treated with a comic irony, as they fight among themselves over such pressing problems as the giving, or not, of a fancy dress ball. Occupying the same house, but a different world, is the mysterious Jean, who keeps his distance from the other inmates and keeps his affairs completely to himself; and the young Hedwige, who has fallen desperately in love with a young man she has met only once. She is similar to Adrienne of *The Closed Garden* in her tendency to fix, compulsively and exclusively, on a chance male as the only possible means of escaping from an oppressive life. Her relations with the young Gaston are identical with Adrienne's relations with Dr. Maurecourt—entirely imaginary. Pressured by half-conscious drives, both young ladies seize mentally on a man met by chance, invest him with all sorts of virtues and attributes, and build their emotional lives around their self-created "lovers," who are of course unaware of the girls' single-minded passions.

The situation is somewhat more complicated in *The Transgressor*, however, in that Gaston has another impassioned admirer, one with whom he does have real relationship—the mysterious Jean, who turns out to be a victim of that "impossible love" which looms so large in Green's life and writing. Jean lives an "underground" existence, carrying on, so we are led to infer, a series of covert affairs with young men of the village, especially with Gaston, a contemptible young fellow, in the business solely for the money. Jean, under threat of exposure and arrest, flees to Italy, where he eventually commits suicide. But not before writing to Hedwige, of whom he is genuinely fond, warning her in roundabout terms of the nature of Gaston and of the hopelessness of her attachment to the vicious young man. Hedwige, unable to break free from her passion, even when she finally realizes the full meaning of what Jean has tried to communicate to her, soon follows Jean in suicide in order to end her suffering and hide the disgrace of her life.

Jean, as it so happens, is not the only person in the story to warn Hedwige of dangers her obsessed young life was leading her into. On two occasions she has dreams, sometimes featuring a handsome Gaston in thinly veiled erotic episodes, and sometimes a humble, rather shoddily dressed man, unknown to the girl, who in the magic of dreams makes various precious objects in Hedwige's room disappear. Green himself, in his introduction to the French edition of the novel, explains the meaning of the stranger in the dream: the man is trying to make her renounce, first, all her earthly goods, and then, a love destined to failure: "That man is Christ, but she does not know it."

Green has some interesting things to tell us in that introduction to a novel which was, curiously enough, begun at the end of 1937, abandoned in 1938 and left in a drawer until January, 1955, when it was taken up again, finished in six months, and published in 1956. He says, by way of explaining the long interruption in the writing, that religious problems turned him increasingly away from the subject of *Le Malfaiteur*, religious problems which are suggested in this work only by the Christ figure in the dream. There were also other reasons why he was willing to leave a hundred pages of manuscript lying untouched for nearly twenty years: the turbulent times, the strikes and threats of war, made him doubt the possibility of publishing this particular work. So he started another novel, which he published in 1940 (*Varouna*, or *Then Shall the Dust Return*), which was a "violent effort to escape the present world, whereas *Le Malfaiteur* plunged me into it." Green then goes on to compare the novel with his play *Sud*, which has a comparable subject. In the play Regina loves Ian as Hedwige loves Gaston, neither with the least hope of success, and for the same reason. But there is a difference in the two stories: "in the play, as in the novel, the two women inspire only respect or pity, but the man in *Sud* commits no other fault than to rebel against destiny, whereas in *Le Malfaiteur* the object of an unhappy passion that leads the heroine to suicide is an insignificant creature completely unworthy of the love he inspires." True, and Green underlines a more important difference when he points out that in *Sud*, "I was obliged to see the subject through the eyes of the hero, while in *Malfaiteur* I tried to understand the tragedy of an impossible love such as the woman would conceive it."[7]

But why did Green return to a manuscript in 1955 which he had abandoned in 1938? Green explains that he did not want to leave any work unfinished, but the main reason was quite different: he wanted to "bring to serious readers' attention one of the most tragic aspects of carnal life in our modern world, tragic because it engages, often in a violent fashion, the entire emotional life and touches gravely on the spiritual life." He deplores the avalanche of obscene books of the last dozen years which deal only physically and therefore superficially with the subject. (He reiterates this objection in his preface to *Sud*.) He personally cannot consider any human problem except in its relation to religion—and the Church is silent on this one.[8] Green, as we have seen, chose not to remain silent, and in most of his works, especially the later ones, the problem of homosexual love is present—centrally in *The Transgressor*, *L'Autre Sommeil*, and *Sud*, less centrally but still crucially in *Moira* and *Each in His Darkness*. In each case—with the exception of Gaston in *The Transgressor* and Max in *Each in His Darkness*, who are shady characters using sexual perversion for their own profit—the problem is treated sympathetically, since the afflicted young men are seen as victims, not just of biological maladjustment, but of social and temporal maladjustments as well. At another time and in another place, the point is made, these painful problems would not be problems at all. As Green puts it in *Terre Lointaine*, thinking of the pre-Christian Greeks, "in any case *they* would have understood me." This point was made with special poignancy in the play *Sud*, which, despite its historical setting, is autobiographical in its characterizations.

III   *The Novelist in the Theater:* Sud

For many years the prominent French actor Louis Jouvet had encouraged Green to try his hand at writing plays. He had insisted that Green was basically a "man of the theater" and had pointed out that the dialogues in the novels were those of a playwright. But Green was fully aware that the fictional dialogues—presented as they are in a context of description, analysis, interior monologue, and other such expositional devices—are very different in their nature and effect from dramatic dialogues on stage, which must stand largely by themselves. He has pointed out that a given story would be presented very differently in a novel than it would be in a play.[9]

Nevertheless, Green admits that, in composing a play, his manner of creation is the same as in writing a novel: he works without a plan or outline—he prefers to create characters and allow them to more or less work out their own destinies. He states that he did not see the plot of *Sud* in its entirety when he began writing; rather, he "watched" the characters appear—first a young man in uniform, then a young lady, then an older woman, and

so on, until the closing lines of the first act. He was somewhat
startled by those lines and wondered if he had hidden his subject from himself without realizing it. It was only with the
meeting of Ian and Erik at the end of the first act—when Ian
gazes with silent intensity at the handsome newcomer—that
the plot asserted itself. From that moment on, says Green, Ian
is caught up in his personal drama—"the drama of a love pronounced anathema by society, and he ran to his doom."[10]

Sud, which was written in 1952 and first presented on stage in
1953, was published with a rather unusual preface by Green: he
not only tells his readers why he wrote the play but also gives
a summary of the plot, as if he were unsure of the play's capacity
to convey its message to its audience. If this was indeed Green's
assumption, there is reason to believe that he was not entirely
wrong. The *New Yorker* critic Genet wrote in 1953 that the
audience did not know what the play was about,[11] and a scholar
who has made a study of the critical reaction to Green's works
says that, despite some defenders, all of Green's plays baffled the
critics and were generally not well received.[12] But before considering some reasons for this confusion, let us hear Green's own
views on *Sud*. He says he wrote the play in reaction against a
"literature of unequal quality," beginning about 1925, which had
spoiled, in his opinion, a serious and noble subject by situating
it almost entirely on the physical level. He is referring here to
the subject of homosexual love which he insists must, like any
other form of love, be seen in its complete emotional and
spiritual context.[13] He then gives us the principal theme of the
play:

On the eve of the War of Secession, an American Lieutenant has a
revelation of his own deepest nature and of a most imperious love
on first seeing a young man whom he knows only by his name. He
is seized by a fear which almost amounts to panic, but which he
succeeds in mastering. Seeking to avoid his destiny, he asks the
hand of a young girl, Angelina, to whom he had previously paid
slight attention. However, it is all too clear that he is not in love
with her, and three persons tell him this, each in his own way: first
Angelina herself, then her father, and finally Jimmy, a boy of fourteen
who speaks with all candor. The lieutenant Wiczewski tries to
confess his passion to the young man who is its object, but he is
not entirely successful in this, and re-enacting the gesture of one
of his ancestors in an analogous circumstance, he tries to kill Eric

MacClure. In order to provoke him into a duel, he insults and slaps him. However, at the moment of combat he offers himself as victim to the man whom he has made his enemy and dies by his hand.[14]

Green further states that "the sin of Ian Wiczewski is not his having loved Erik MacClure, but rather his having inflicted cruel suffering on the lady whose pardon he then asks. In no way does he feel himself to be a pariah or leper. As he will say to himself an hour before having himself killed: 'I am not ashamed, but I feel alone.'" Green adds in conclusion: "In order to preserve in this play all the gravity inherent in the problems it raises, I have tried to give it the general form of tragedy. Someone has remarked that, on stage, my characters exchange confidences at a distance of five meters. That is, precisely, the tone that I have sought."

Regarding this last remark about the distance between characters, it is apparent that the relationship between Ian and Erik is set in a context of more generalized human relationships and the problems of communication, or noncommunication, which they pose: relations between members of the family, projected against the larger screen of a divided North and South on the eve of war; between white masters and black slaves; between various individuals emotionally and amorously involved with each other—and in each case there is a tragic abyss between them. The gulf which separates Ian from Erik is but one of many intrapersonal gulfs, which places Ian's problem *within* a group of comparable problems instead of isolating it as something special and alien to human experience. But Green seems to be implying that persons suffering from the "impossible love" are subjected to a kind of "double jeopardy": the scene where Ian tries vainly to make Erik guess his feelings toward him—which Erik is incapable of doing—illustrates doubly the impossibility of communication, for to the natural solitude of the human heart is added another barrier, that of a passion without hope, impossible to declare. This serves to erect two impenetrable circles of isolation around him. Ian (in terms which Green himself will use in his later autobiographical work, *Terre Lointaine*),[15] trying to tell Erik of his passion, says that he knows full well that he can never speak to Erik of what he is most concerned about: "In other times, in other places, perhaps, but this evening, between these walls, no. Everything here closes my mouth."

In a similar way, Denis tries to enlighten Claude in *L'Autre Sommeil;* Simon fails to communicate to Joseph Day in *Moira;* and Angus tries to make his feelings clear to Wilfred in *Each in His Darkness.* It is a love that not only cannot be realized, it cannot even be named; for in our culture, in our time, it would not be "understood."

These dramatized experiences, as I have indicated, have their counterparts in Green's autobiographical writings, and it is interesting to consider the parallels between Green and his character Ian Wiczewski. There is a similarity between the situations of Poland and the American South, in that the Polish Ian and southerner Green are in a sense both aliens, and they come from countries whose cultures no longer have autonomous existence, both being dominated by a "foreign" power; they both feel a noninvolvement in current troubles, the clashes of political and national forces; each is totally absorbed in his personal problems, an intense inner war within himself, which is merely counterpointed by the external conflict of arms.

It is no wonder that this play, which can be understood only in the context of Green's other writings, baffled its audiences. As presented on stage, it would appear to lack a central point of view, a central character, and thematic unity. Dialogue often seems directionless. As one critic has put it, Green, as novelist, sees and presents characters from the inside—they are not projected objectively and autonomously on stage. Seen from without they do not always make sense, or they are misunderstood: the homosexual problem was missed by most audiences—they were thrown off the track by Regina's love for Ian and by Ian's spurious proposal of marriage to Angelina.[16] But the play *does* have form and unity: the relationship between Ian and Erik is one of a number of parallel relationships, each resulting in failure of communication, but such a multiplicity of themes can scarcely be grasped by a theater audience. The play is too long and has too many characters; motivation is not clearly indicated; and the all-important theme of destiny is overshadowed by subplots. The play can be read and appreciated by someone familiar with Green and his other writings but not as an autonomous piece of theater.[17]

IV   L'Ennemi

In one of his other plays, *L'Ennemi* (*The Enemy*, 1954), Green returns to a favorite and persistent theme: the conflict between the two worlds, the seen and the unseen, the realms of body and soul, with their eternally irreconcilable demands, and the resultant tension, inescapable yet intolerable, which creates, in Green, an intense longing for the beyond—the absolute.

The action of *L'Ennemi* takes place in 1785, four years before the end of the Ancien Régime. Pierre, the bastard son of the Silleranges family, has just returned to the château where live his half-brother Philippe and his sister-in-law Elizabeth, along with his other half-brother Jacques, who is secretly the lover of Elizabeth. Five years earlier, Pierre, though devoted to a life of debauchery, had suddenly retired from the world and entered a monastery. But one day a beautiful young lady had presented herself at the gates, and Pierre had left the monastery to follow her. After a brief affair, he has now returned to the family château.

Elizabeth believes herself to be emancipated from Christian beliefs, but in spite of the freedom of mind and manners she allows herself, she is dying of melancholy in the depths of the provinces and feels nothing but emptiness in what passes, in those parts, for social diversions. Her husband Philippe, it appears, has been rendered impotent by an accident, and Pierre guesses what kind of a man it would take to attain the favors of the unhappy Elizabeth, who is scarcely content with her current lover, Jacques. He plays the part to perfection, appeals to her need for intellectual nourishment, and succeeds in taking her away from Jacques. In listening to Pierre's brilliant conversations, which have such an impact on her mind and emotions, Elizabeth changes completely. She abandons her "libertinage" and aspires to the absolute, whose presence she has sensed behind the fragile veil of this world. The curtain falls on the first act, just at the moment when Pierre has made his brilliant conquest of his sister-in-law. He bursts into laughter by way of announcing his victory over his half-brother, who has just lost the mistress he had stolen from another.

Philippe, meanwhile, suffers as he has always suffered from the torments of his impotency, guessing his wife's infidelity. Always suspicious, he spies on Elizabeth with a certain gloomy

pleasure, savoring his jealousy as a torture both exquisite and
intolerable. The humiliated Jacques is no less bitter than the
husband and vows revenge, evolving a plot to rid the world of
Pierre.

But Pierre, just like the Elizabeth he has so greatly influenced,
undergoes a change of character. He is snared in his own game
and finds that he has fallen hopelessly in love with Elizabeth,
who is no longer interested in physical intimacies, having been
caught up in her vision of a superior way of life. Once having
seen the mysterious light of spirituality, she rejects the banalities
of this crude material world. Divine love will be her only love.
But she understands that her happiness on the human level is
threatened by the demanding voice of the spiritual, which
comes to her from some unknown beyond; and she sees it as,
in this terrestrial sense, the enemy. Pierre, on his part, rebels
against the invisible power dominating his mistress, and he turns,
in another about-face, toward the Prince of Darkness. In the
subsequent conversations between the two lovers, we are aware
that the Divine Spirit speaks and that the Devil replies: the
ancient drama of body and soul is being acted out.

Elizabeth, fully aware of what is happening to Pierre, becomes
fearful for his life, sensing a threat of death hovering about
him. Though she knows nothing of the vengeful plot that
Jacques has devised, she begs Pierre to flee the château without
delay. He refuses, remains at Silleranges, and is killed. This
turn of events is too much for the fragilely balanced mentality
of Elizabeth; she becomes deranged, and in the final scene she
believes she sees, all about her, the flames of divine love, flames
which in an earlier scene she had seen in a vivid dream, a
dream so real that she could remember every detail but could
not find the terms with which to describe it to the incredulous
Pierre. But the gist of her vision is that the flames are not just the
vision of divine spirit; they are also *her*; she *was* the flames; and
they are, at the same time, the spirit of the universe: love. She
felt that in her dream she had awakened from the nightmare of
life and saw reality for the first time. The physical world was a
lie, and its pleasures were nothing compared to the ecstasy she
experienced in her vision of the divine flames. That was her
destiny: "We are creatures of fire.... Behind the thin partition
of time burned the paradise of eternity." This rhapsodic invoca-

tion to the spiritual world of fire is repeated at the end of the play, when Elizabeth, her mind shattered by the death of Pierre, continues to talk to her departed lover who, to her, is merely hiding behind the "great doorway that leads to God," and behind that door is eternally whispered what only she and Pierre had heard: "You and I alone have heard it."

All of Green's works are, to varying degrees, confessions, and this play is especially so. He has admitted in his *Journal* that he cannot view it objectively, "since I am on the inside." Elizabeth, he tells us, "is a reflection of what I am myself [*"Le feu est ma patrie"*][18] and I find myself in *The Enemy* much more than in my Journal or novels." As Saint Jean puts it, in this play—Green's château of the soul—he has hidden a great secret. But this secret, if not totally revealed, is intelligible to readers of his other works and of his *Journal,* where the same struggle between body and soul, between the terrestrial and the divine, is carried on in the "battlefield" of Green's own person.

V L'Ombre

Green's third play, *L'Ombre* (The Shadow, 1956), does not appear to be so immediately drawn from the author's own life or personal writings. It resembles in theme one of the Greek dramas of the Orestes myth, with overtones of *Othello,* in which the protagonist cannot escape the actions of his past. Remorse and reminders of past sins return in inescapable forms to plague and punish the perpetrator until he finally passes judgment upon and executes himself. For in this drama, the Furies are not transformed into Eumenides to alleviate the burden of Orestes' conscience and bring him peace. The central character, Philip Anderson, cannot efface the memory of the tragic circumstances under which his first wife met her death, and he cannot escape the torment of remorse. It appears that, being convinced of his wife's infidelity, Philip had arranged, with the assistance of a friend, for his wife to fall "accidentally" to her death from a high cliff. The "friend" first comes back, in person, to act as a "'conscience" for Philip; after the friend's death, the friend's son takes up the role, insinuating himself into Philip's household. By this time, Philip, even though he has taken a second wife, has become obsessed by the memory of his first wife's murder,

and, on learning that she was innocent of any infidelity, he goes
to the same cliff and hurls himself over. Unable to escape from
the shadow *(l'ombre)* which the memory of his wife cast over
him, he went to join her.

Green has written no other plays. He returned to the writing
of fiction and straight autobiography, and this was doubtless a
wise decision. While his plays are not without a certain merit,
they do not hold much appeal for general audiences. Green's
experience with the theater tends to prove, as in the case of
Henry James, that the ability to compose highly "dramatic"
scenes in a work of fiction does not mean that an author can
readily transfer that ability to composing for the theater. Green
needs the fuller context of narrative prose if his themes and
characterizations are to become meaningful to his audience.

CHAPTER 6

The Later Novels:
Entrapment and Escape

I Moira

THE major theme of Green's later writings—the tragic results of man's inability to reconcile the drives of the flesh with his need for a spiritual life—is further developed in *Moira* (1950, 1959)[1] and *Each in His Darkness* (*Chaque Homme dans sa Nuit*, 1960, 1961). Each novel deals with a young man in whom the forces of physical lust and spiritual hunger are locked in deadly combat, each force striving to destroy the other. The young man feels himself to be the arena in which the struggle must be resolved, and it is he who is destroyed, physically at least, while gaining at the end the possibility of spiritual salvation. The two novels can be seen as companion pieces: one depicts the struggles of a fanatical puritan beset by a physical lust he cannot understand; the other portrays a dedicated lecher who cannot suppress or avoid the urgings of his spiritual nature. It is interesting to note that it is the latter—Wilfred in *Each in His Darkness*—who most clearly achieves spiritual salvation, perhaps because, though an impenitent sinner, he comes to recognize his spiritual urgings for what they are, to understand his sinful nature, and to transcend it. The power of religious spirit in him, far from being extinguished by his sexual excesses, is progressively strengthened. His associates sense this spiritual power in him and come to him for aid. In fact, the novel appears to be less about Wilfred's individual triumph over sin than about the capacity of spirituality to persevere under the most adverse conditions and ultimately to overwhelm the forces of darkness which conspire to crush it.

The case of Joseph Day is a less promising one, however. While he ultimately yields to secular authority to do penance for his sins, his understanding of his condition and his capacity for redemption are relatively limited. The ill-fated hero of *Moira* is a robust rustic straight from the hills, who has come to a large sophisticated university to pursue studies and encounter experiences for which he is hopelessly unprepared. As he stands in the vestibule of the boarding house, being coolly surveyed by the worldly landlady, he fairly exudes a sense of alienation, an awareness that he is out of his element. He is "different" from the people around him, and this difference is dramatized by his physical appearance: his skin is milky white, his eyes are black; his hair is flaming red, a red that is echoed by the landlady's lipstick and later on, by the lipstick and crimson dress of Joseph's nemesis, Moira.

Joseph, though ill at ease in his new environment, is far from passive. His puritan soul is repelled by the depravity of university life, as he sees it, and he comes to detest most of the students who seem addicted to carnal pastimes. He rebels against university life and his own repressed compulsion to join that life; for he too is obsessed by what Green calls *"la loi charnelle"* and fights to resist it. His buried sexual desires are in open conflict with the puritan surface of his life, and the resulting tensions become insupportable: he is a miserably unhappy young man, and his religious self is horrified to discover that the unresolved tensions of existence are driving him increasingly toward violence—a hatred and tendency toward violence which will ultimately make a murderer of him. "I hate the sexual instinct," says Green in his *Journal*, and this phrase echoes throughout the novel, where it carries over to everyone associated, in Joseph's mind, with sexuality.

Green admits that he was much like Joseph Day when he was his age and that he has told the story largely "like it was," without benefit of hindsight or revisions of more mature judgment. Like the Green of the autobiographies, Joseph Day is repelled not only by the virile antics of his fellow students but by sexuality in any form: he avoids looking at the campus statues, and, after discovering "licentious" passages in *Romeo and Juliet*, he refuses to read Shakespeare. He is another of Green's characters who dress and undress in the dark, repelled by their own bodies. His attempts to reform his fellows earn him the satiric title of "Exterminating Angel," and his holier-than-thou attitude eventually provokes his comrades into taking appropriate revenge. They plot the downfall of this Saint John the Baptist who poses as the paragon of all virtue and chastity. Joseph was already much aware of the seductive young Moira, having met her on occasions and having even slept in her bed while she was away on an extended visit, but he was not prepared to find her planted in his room one night. Moira, well known and much appreciated by the local boys, is a willing accomplice in the plot to bring about the fall of Saint John, who had so far rejected her obvious charms. But now, with the door key slipped into her décolleté bosom, her mouth "red as an open wound," seductively dressed and decorated with bracelets, and exuding a head-swimming perfume, Moira proves too much for Joseph's puritanical self. His repressed lust overwhelms him. He succumbs, but only after considerable twisting and turning to avoid falling, while Moira hovers patiently, as sure of the outcome as a spider watching the helpless struggles of a fly in her web. After the night of sex, in the light of day, the outraged puritan in Joseph reasserts itself, and he reacts with vengeful violence against the cause of his fall. He strangles Moira, and then, horrified by what he has done in his frenzy, he tries to hide the evidence. At dawn, he buries the body, under a blanket of white snow in a grove of nearby trees. He then tries to flee, but he is brought back, through the combined influence of his conscience and the persuasion of one of his acquaintances who had been involved in the Moira plot. He gives himself up to the police.

On one occasion Green had written in his *Journal:* "There is a novel to be written which could be called *The Novel of the Redhead [Le Roman du Roux].* The redhead is a solitary." This comment supports our awareness, already well established by the narrative itself, that the story is essentially symbolic and that color is a large part of the symbolism. The basic colors are spelled out, as we have seen, by the opening pages: red, black, and white; and these colors work to emphasize the element of fatality that runs through the story. Joseph's flaming hair, standing in such blatant contradiction to his white skin, objectifies the ardent and violent nature of the young man as it struggles with his religious convictions. Joseph's whiteness, which brings to mind the pure white skin of John the Baptist who endeavored (with more success) to evade the wily charms of Salomé, is supported by his name, Day, and the whiteness of the snow under which Moira's body will be buried, conceals, in its surface purity, the carnal reality that lies beneath. The startling red of his hair is not only clearly representative of Joseph's difference, his isolation, and of the ardor and violence that lurk beneath the whiteness, but is also related, as has been suggested, to the sexuality of Moira—first foreshadowed in the disturbingly "excessive" lipstick on the landlady, interestingly named Mrs. Dare, and then centered in Moira's dress, worn on the night that Joseph's fate overtakes him. For it must strike most readers that Moira's name, which is Greek for "fate," could not have been chosen at random (though Green, in conversation, says that he happened on the charming "Irish" name by chance).

This interweaving of a strong sense of inevitability, of personal fatality, is characteristic of most of Green's novels, and it is handled masterfully in *Moira:* the reader is prepared to accept as inevitable the murder of the girl by Joseph Day. Even though she appears rarely in the narrative, her disturbing presence is felt throughout. We *see* her only twice, but she lives vividly in Joseph's imagination, a most lively imagination, as it turns out, which dwells broodingly on ideas and images which he does not fully understand himself but which we, as readers, are privileged to grasp. We note, for example, that Moira's cigarette case, symbol of her debauchery, recurs frequently. Indeed, one critic sees Joseph's imagination as his fate; that is, it is his *imaginative* concept of Moira and not her reality that pushes him to his disastrous fate.[2] There is something to this, but it is also true that her physical reality, as presented overwhelmingly to him in the night in his room, demolishes his moral resistance.

Green, however, as author, *tells* us very little about the characters; we learn, or infer, much about Joseph, and through him about the others, by interpreting for ourselves the disheveled thoughts, feelings, and images that pass through Joseph's mind. We learn that he is passionate, impatient, and something of an untamed animal despite his religious training, and we learn that he is hostile to the world as he finds it—not through Green's comments but through the gestures and actions of Joseph himself. We observe the slow rise of the crucial emotion, sexual desire, from its buried depths to its open assertion, and we grasp

Joseph's confusion as to its direction and object. He becomes conscious of his sexual desire for Moira but never for another important character in the story, named Praileau, an elegant, sneeringly handsome young student who takes certain perverse joy in baiting Joseph, teasing him for his red hair and aloof manner, until Joseph is driven to challenge him to physical combat. Joseph comes to hate Praileau and, in his need for revenge, turns a wrestling match into attempted murder. Joseph is horrified by the discovery of his own capacity for ultimate violence, and Praileau, recognizing this capacity in his antagonist, openly tells Joseph that he is a "murderer."

In his epigraph to his play *Sud*, Green quotes Aristotle that "the purification of a dangerous passion by a vehement liberation" is natural to victims of intolerable tensions and inner conflicts. Green himself, recalling that the imaginary games he played as a boy usually involved violence and murder, says, "I realize that my gentle nature corresponded very little with the studied ferocity of this mental game, but I cannot conceal from myself that, under my apparent gentleness, there breathed and stirred extreme violence. With time, all this passed into my novels."[3] And from the murderer Guéret in *The Dark Journey* to the murderer Joseph Day in *Moira* we find this to be true: the source of the violence and killing is sexual. Out of frustrated sexual desire for Angèle, Guéret tries to kill her and does kill an inadvertent passerby; and out of sexual desire—confused, undirected, and unconscious—Joseph tries to kill Praileau. A similar sexual attraction-repulsion is described by Green in *To Leave Before Dawn*, where he reminisces about a fight he had with a fellow classmate: "I threw myself with all my might on my opponent, and together we rolled to the foot of the platform. Such fury possessed us both that we never dreamt of crying out and, in the deepest silence, did the best we could to kill each other. Now that I can see these things more lucidly, it is clear that we unwittingly freed ourselves of a kind of amorous rage that assumed the face of hatred."

It is also clear that the same amorous rage consumes Joseph in his battle with Praileau, though of course he does not recognize it as such, any more than he recognizes the homosexual advances made to him by his friend Simon, who subsequently commits suicide. For Joseph is victimized by an undifferentiated sexual desire that is rendered unintelligible to him by his eighteen years of ignorance of carnal life, and he fails also to see that in killing Moira it is probably Praileau he is killing. Or, even more probably, Moira and Praileau have become so confused in his mind and feelings that he is killing both of them, as principles of physical lust that must be destroyed. And so the homicidal instinct which was linked to sexual instinct in the first pages of the story comes to its inevitable and preordained conclusion.

II   Each in His Darkness

The central character of *Each in His Darkness (Chaque Homme dans sa Nuit*, 1961)[4] is a young man, a humble shirt salesman in a large store, who, behind a façade of modesty and virtue, lives a life of vigorous licentiousness. Wilfred goes from woman to woman, picking them up at random, enjoying the obvious attraction which they feel for him. He does not, however, lose track of the perils to which he is exposing himself, for he still adheres, spasmodically at least, to a demanding religious faith. He tries to be a man of the flesh without giving up his puritanical Catholicism. Like so many of Green's characters, Wilfred is a man divided against himself; he is a battleground for what he conceives to be the forces of good and evil. As Wilfred himself says, he believes in God with all his soul, but his body does not believe. So, before plunging into the lowlife of the town, the low dives where he seeks out his casual partners for the night, he is always careful to remove the little cross he wears around his neck, and it is only after this gesture that the man of pleasure replaces the Christian.

Just as the sexually repressed Joseph Day in *Moira* is repelled by the sight of nude statues, so Wilfred is openly stimulated by them. In fact, at the beginning of the story, his nature is defined by his response to one such statue when, on entering the vestibule of his uncle's mansion, " the first thing to meet his eye was a large and well-nigh naked woman of polished bronze who carried a torch in her fist." Two pages later he returns to view the woman again: "To look at her aroused evil thoughts, those of which you are bound to accuse yourself, but he had had so many since his last confession that one more would make no great difference. He was up to his eyes in mortal sin, and really the woman was beautiful.... The young man looked a little longer at the perfect limbs, at all that flesh. To look meant a sort of happiness mingled with pain, with hunger, something that devastated the heart."

Since women, at least the kind Wilfred associates with, find him to be irresistible, he invariably meets with success, and he goes from woman to woman without, however, knowing love—until the day he meets Phoebe, young wife of his cousin James Knight. This time, in her presence, he discovers with surprise that more than just his senses are moved. He finds himself overwhelmingly in love with the pure young wife and totally devoted to her. The ardent yet scrupulous hero finds that having an affair with a married woman is not in his line. Avoiding even the thought of adultery, he confides to his "friend" Max, a sort of alter ego or "black angel" who seeks to bring unhappiness on those whose religious beliefs inspire in him hatred and spite. It is apparent that Max, at some time in his life, had experienced a spiritual anguish which his faith had not survived; nevertheless, he returns with zest to the problem of the existence of God as if he enjoyed some somber pleasure in the denial. He is visibly interested in Wilfred, but it is the soul he covets in him, the soul he would deliver to the "enemy." He is indeed in the classic tradition of devilish tempters. But Max knows very well that he will not convert a young man whose surface tumults of the senses have never troubled his soul to any great depth. Religion remains always there, just below the surface, running like an underground stream, and Max says wrathfully to the rebel who refuses to follow him: "Your behavior lacks firmness, and in the end you're always ready to say yes to God. That's what's likely to make you bungle the affair [with Phoebe]. Believe me, I'm wise to all these dodges. I've gone through fits of religion." After which he takes up his favorite refrain: faith cannot stand up before desire. Wilfred resists this line of reasoning, but the evil advocate always returns to the attack, without success. And, ironically enough, it is Wilfred's debaucheries that will save him: they lead him, through satiety and disgust, to repentance.

Despite the depravity of his physical life, a spiritual force radiates from Wilfred that attracts other people. They come to him asking for help, and even those who do not share his beliefs sense that the young man has some special religious power. He becomes, unwillingly, a kind of lay priest. One of his friends, Freddie, receives baptism from his hands; and James Knight, his cousin, makes this remark to him: "If you ever lost your faith, you'd blow your brains out." Yet James does not suspect that a "voice" frequently speaks to Wilfred when he is alone, some "other self" whose voice recurs like an insistent refrain throughout the story: "The words left his lips as though someone else had spoken them and so distinctly as to rouse him abruptly from lethargy." "The sound of his voice seemed as strange to him as if someone else had spoken." Once, in a church: "'And what about me?' asked a voice in the innermost part of his being as he marked that Sunday's Mass with a ribbon. Wilfred did not reply. 'I love you,' said the voice. 'There I go, imagining all sorts of things,' thought Wilfred." "At one point, the memory of his visit to the church and his confession flitted through his mind and astounded him: so, you could very easily be two persons." "For a few seconds, he had the feeling, one that was so familiar to him, of having been overtaken by someone more powerful than he."

This voice, his basic religious self, will remain unextinguished throughout his life of debauchery, and it will become, in his final speech, his own voice. He will resist, however, until the end. But until that time, he lives a double life. When his uncle is dying, he calls Wilfred to his bedside, convinced that his nephew better than anyone else can help him make that great crossing over. There follows a scene of curious religious dialogue between the two men, in which Wilfred has to pose as the virtuous believer while knowing in his heart he is the heir, not only to his uncle's money, but to his sensual life as well.

But soon there springs up between Wilfred and Phoebe, young wife of James Knight, a silent and unavowed love, recognized by each, in which no demands are made other than spiritual. Any physical consummation is out of the question: their love is virtually mystical. James Knight, who observes the mutual attraction of the young couple, misunderstands their relationship at first; but he soon comes to see that their love transcends the physical. As for Wilfred, he is astonished at himself: he is no longer the young sinner wallowing in lechery. This transformation also astonishes Max and fills him with hatred: Wilfred has

not eliminated religion from his life, so Max will eliminate
Wilfred.

Desirous of coming to the moral aid of Max, Wilfred seeks
him out and finally finds him in a sort of brothel where Max
turns out to be a kind of male prostitute. A long argument ensues
which ends in Max's becoming enraged to the point of near-
madness. Wilfred sees the futility of his efforts to talk to Max
and suddenly senses the presence of a terrible menace in the
small, sordid room; he fears that Max's anger is going to change
into homicidal fury, and with a pain in his heart, he leaves,
fleeing the trap into which he had fallen. He is possessed by
panic, and he descends the stairway four steps at a time. At the
moment he is passing the threshold of the building, Max points
a revolver at him, at Wilfred who had come to save him. Wilfred
speeds up and leaps out into the street, but a bullet strikes him
down.

Max may be the emissary of death and damnation, but he
is not portrayed as being all of a piece, as bearing only the colors
of the damned. He is a man of violent contrasts, like Wilfred,
and the "sense of the invisible" strikes him at certain moments.
Thus, there escapes from him after he has shot Wilfred, a cry
which one might expect to hear from the lips of a true believer:
"Say you forgive me. . . . Say yes, for the love of Christ!" To
which Wilfred responds his last words, in a scarcely audible
murmur: "Yes."

This novel of faith—or as one critic has put it, this novel "of
faith in faith"—is developed in the uncertainty of its final outcome,
for the spiritual struggle remains in doubt until the very second
when Wilfred lies curled up on the sidewalk.[5]

In this respect, Green has observed: *"Chaque Homme dans
sa Nuit* is related . . . to *Voyageur sur la Terre,* for, at the end
of those two books, rays of light shine under the closed door
[an image which is also used in the play *The Enemy*], and hope
prevails over anguish. I think the critics are right in asserting
that this book constitutes my first optimistic novel. Wilfred
will be saved."[6] He adds:

I have made it clearly understood, I think, that the salvation of
Wilfred is probable, at the very least. On the purely human level,
my character's death is a disaster, since he falls by an assassin's
bullet, but from the point of view of Wilfred himself—granting that

he could have had an opinion—any end which leaves his hope for salvation intact is a death full of light. For from that very instant his entire life took a direction it never had until then. The treasure of faith—he had kept it in spite of everything until the last second. One might wonder what would have become of him if he had lived to a ripe old age instead of dying in the fullness of youth. But that would be another novel, less optimistic perhaps than the one I have written.

Green confesses that, while writing the novel, he did not clearly see its significance. When the novel was completed, and when seeking an appropriate title, Green wondered about the book's meaning:

It was only after writing "the end" at the bottom of the last page that I asked myself about the meaning of this lengthy narrative, for I had yet to find the title. . . . A line from Victor Hugo in a poem re-read by chance seemed to sum up the novel: "Each man in his darkness moves towards his light." The life of each of us has a direction that escapes us. . . . What seems to us today to be muddled, obscure, and confused, will eventually be revealed to us in its essential harmony. Each of us, despite difficulties, vacillations, failures, moves none the less, in a stifling darkness, towards peace. There will finally come the day when, as the Scriptures say, God will wipe away all tears. . . . To be sure, we do not know how our salvation operates, and our lives seem like a novel whose title we cannot discover, but God provides that title.[7]

III Conclusion: Attempts to Escape

All of Green's works are expressions of the need to escape the suffering of human life. He has confessed that "My greatest sin will be not to have been willing to accept the human condition." This describes many of Green's characters, *"les réfractaires,"* who refuse to share the fates of the *"englués"*—literally, those "glued," as by a limed twig—caught, trapped, taken in. How to extricate oneself? Human reason is not a sufficient instrument for piercing the mystery of man's existence or for escaping his condition: "What makes the greatness of man is not his reason—it is his knowledge of things which lie beyond that reason," his capacity for recognizing the "impasses of intellectual illusion." Monsieur Fruges, for example, in *If I Were You,* is intelligent and knowledgeable; he recognizes the necessity for resistance and revolt: "He was not long in scenting danger, the greatest danger that could possibly threaten him at the moment, that of becoming resigned to his fate." For him it would be necessary to revive the nearly extinct embers of religious faith, but that would require a miracle, one for which he begged under the gray vaults of his church, a miracle comparable to that of Lazarus: the resurrection of his soul, something he almost no longer believed in or knew how to ask for. He had a soul, but it had lost what was unique and essential to it—which was *not* its subtle faculties of analysis and its intellectual comprehension of the universe. How to flee from one's solitude, how to clear the walls of the human condition and liberate oneself from existential anguish? How to escape from oneself?

Most attempts to escape are abortive. In *The Strange River,* the egotist Philip thinks to escape from himself and only finds himself in another person, his son. The father of the narrator of *L'Autre Sommeil* tries to find in his business office and in his study "the oblivion that others attained through debauchery," but he did not find consolation sufficient to avoid suicide. However, several of Green's characters struggle against the "chains of reality" with such force that they achieve, temporarily at least, a sense of escape.

The most immediate, elementary, and efficacious way to shatter one's imprisoning routine is to return to the instinctual life. Serge, in *Midnight,* is sort of a primal type, the incarnation of sexual instinct in its most attractive form ("it dazzles the heart by jarring the senses"). He is a physical and nonrational reaction to Monsieur Edme's world of "pure spirit." In *Moira,* Joseph Day is also, in some respects, a primitive, a young untamed animal. The tragedy lies in the fact that this wildly fanatical puritan tries to reject with all his soul the brute imperatives of his instincts.

An uncontrolled instinct is conducive to the quest for physical pleasure. This may take the form, for some persons, of a search for the absolute, consciously or unconsciously. Green laments in his *Journal*: "Does our body never weary of craving the same thing? . . . There have always been but two types of men I have truly well understood, the mystic and debauchee, because both, each in his own way, fly to extremes and seek the absolute." But "pleasure does not lead to anything. It wants to be an end in itself and that is a role it plays poorly—it is the ape of the absolute. The most it can do is to achieve the illusion of annihilation."[8]

Pleasure of the senses can seem a temporary solution to ennui and human solitude; but, for a man possessing a sense of mysticism, "there is something horrible about pleasure." This is the substance of *Moira*. In pleasure "it is not the body that is culpable, but rather the soul that consents. How, being spirit, can it consent to what it detests? But the fact is there: the voluptuary prepares the bed of the unbeliever,"[9] and eroticism invariably engenders suffering, horror, violence, death. Manuel in *The Dreamer* throws himself on the Vicomtesse "like a beast," and after an encounter more frightening than pleasurable, he finds that his mistress is dead in his arms (a dream, but a dream more vivid, more real, than reality). He himself dies shortly afterward. In *Midnight,* young Elizabeth, violated by Serge, abandons herself to the abyss and dies soon after her lover. Angèle in *Dark Journey* is attacked and mutilated and left for dead by the impassioned Guéret—and neither escapes his individual solitude. When sensuality overtakes Joseph Day, in the form of Moira, he succumbs to the girl's physical attraction but the next morning strangles her, after which, deciding not to try to escape, he gives himself up to the police and, at the same time, to his fate.

Another and related form of escape is that of sadism, the sadism of those who must inflict suffering in order to believe in their own existence. Cruelty, like purity, is a kind of "refusal." Monsieur Edme, before becoming a prophet of the immaterial, had filled his life with "small malevolent joys." He was responsible, among other things, for the suicide of Elizabeth's mother, following which "he experienced the happiness of making suffer the only person who interested him." He decides to find his daughter "with the idea of bringing her up as I wished and to rediscover in this child something of the emotions which her mother had aroused in me." Manuel's aunt in *The Dreamer* experiences, at the bedside of her sick nephew, an "atrocious satisfaction" in the presence of his physical suffering. The father in *The Closed Garden* is a case of rather unconscious sadism when he forces his sick daughter to get out of bed and compels Adrienne to play a hated game of cards, but with him it is not a "liberating" cruelty as it is with Madame Grosgeorges.

It is in *The Dark Journey* that we find the most developed portrait of sadism, in Madame Grosgeorges. Bored and frustrated,
she takes vengeance on life by humiliating others. In striking
her son, she enjoys his tears and hopes for some new transgression
on his part as pretext for a new punishment. She detests the child
who reminds her of her hated husband, who is the sign of her
servitude, since she is incapable of abandoning him, of fleeing.
The child is part of that order of things imposed on her without
her consent. Whenever the child is sick, she cares for him solici-
tously but consumed with a ferocious joy. She does not know
what she hopes for. She experiences "hours of perfect satisfaction" on hearing that two crimes had been committed in town
and she enjoys the sense of evil. She reads and rereads zealously
the detailed descriptions of crimes in the newspaper. She gives
refuge to the criminal, Guéret, and feels vaguely drawn to him
personally because she suspects the worst about him. She considers letting him escape; she excites false hopes in him; and
she finally delivers him, indirectly, to the police. Guéret "ought
to have guessed the instincts that possessed her the day he had
seen her strike her son with such passionate calm." He says to
her: "I ought to have known that you would betray me. You
wouldn't turn a hair if your own son's head was being cut off.
You are not a woman, you are a monster, and you have only
come to laugh at my agony." Madame Grosgeorges, having failed
in her efforts to escape from herself, shoots herself. "In the
groans that came from her lips he caught the words: 'Finish me
off. I don't want to live anymore.'" She survives—no doubt to
continue her miserable and absurd existence, immured within
herself.

Also in *The Dark Journey*, Madame Londe displays less culpable, but none the less interesting tendencies toward sadism.
Intensely curious, avid for power and authority, she lacks the
bitterness, the power of hatred, of Madame Grosgeorges. But she
also seeks to transcend her situation by humiliating others and
in dominating and controlling her dozen clients, with the aid of
her informer, Angèle. She enjoys treating them like bad school-
boys as they eat literally at her feet. But she is not happy in her
dominance: "If she could not bear not to see them in this state
of moral bondage, her unsatisfied soul found emptiness, even in
the hour of her triumph. Actually, she possessed what takes the

place of intelligence among civilized people, namely, a deep
insight into human beings and things. Although this prevented
her from being happy, she did not have the strength of mind to
suppress it, and she had relapsed into the melancholy by which
her whole life was consumed."

Reveries and hallucinations are also forms of escape, and they
are preferred by the timid, the introspective, and the solitary—
those who (like Adrienne Mesurat) lack the intellectual and
moral resources for action. At first, dreams appears to be an
innocuous refuge from the harshness of life. But from dreams
one moves to waking dreams and to hallucinations. These are not
just a purely novelistic invention, says Green in his *Journal*: at
Valenciennes, "some peasants said they had seen men emerging
from a flying saucer. I made a note of it because this hallucination indicates something of the color of our times."[10] Even
Adrienne, the petite bourgeoise of small imagination, can take
refuge in a world she creates in order to escape from another.
Trapped in the hell of a provincial salon, she creates an imaginary
world so that Dr. Maurecourt can be present in her life. As
Jeanne writes in her journal in *Then Shall the Dust Return*:
"Has it never entered anyone's mind that all of Hell could be
contained in a provincial drawing room?" In *The Strange River*
Henriette, alienated from her husband by his wealth and his
inadequacy, secretly meets with a man who attracts her because he is both skinny and poor (husband Philip is vain
about his physique; he is fearful of growing fat; and he is
wealthy through no efforts of his own). Henriette finds a certain
pleasure in the imaginary games she plays—the "imaginary path"
she has mapped out which leads her to her lover. For,

like all people whom the world has not succeeded in making happy,
she sought within herself for the elements of her happiness. She
played at life in the same way that children play at soldiers or
brigands, and nothing in her life seemed more real to her than this
imaginary path which cut across other people's paths, becoming
something confused with them, now parting from them and joining
them again, but remaining, in spite of everything, quite distinct.

But the "avenues of revery" are "the preferred promenade
of the devil."[11] Green's characters who break with reality follow
a highly dangerous course. Their efforts, usually catastrophic,

end in almost every case in the dissolution of personality. In *Midnight,* Monsieur Edme, a nocturnal creature, lives a perpetual illusion. He plunges into a kind of nirvana but not without seeking support of his "faithful entourage." As Monsieur Bernard says of his tyrannical brother, Monsieur Edme: "And this charlatan has seduced all the others with his hypocritical kindness and his moralizing. He's persuaded them that life is unbearable except in this tottering house, miles from everything but close to him, so close to him that he cannot feel the horror of his solitude. And every night, in the fear that his authority will relax and these people will *wake up* and rebel, he repeats the lies he has told them the day before, and soothes their fears and over-rides their objections." Monsieur Edme's enterprise ends, of course, in tragedy.

In *The Dreamer,* Manuel, ugly timid, and sickly, living in a world as closed as that of Emily and Adrienne, seeks to escape reality by immersing himself in a world of dreams. But the dream world is also horrible. Manuel's sufferings have so far penetrated his subconscious that the artificial paradise he evokes contains the horrors and pains of the real world he lives in. The example of the "visionary" shows that perfect sublimation is almost impossible. The tyranny exercised by the unconscious condemns in advance the constructions of the imagination.

In *Then Shall the Dust Return* we see a variation on the theme of man's efforts to penetrate the "unreal." Bertrand Lombard "was a mystic astray in a world of sensuality and seeking to escape by means of magic from the hell that he had, as it were, made with his own hands." Anxious to escape at any price, he delivers himself into the hands of his cousin Eustace Croche, whose cabalistic jargon "asked of the Devil what he would not have dared to ask of God." He died "because he was unable to believe in a falsehood that might have brought him several years of enjoyment. His conscience killed him." And in *If I Were You,* Fabian tries to escape from himself in the material sense, to move outside his physical "limits"; but he discovers that even with aid of the Devil, one cannot escape *this* world.

Escape from reality often leads to madness. In *L'Autre Sommeil*: "The reason has nothing more to do in a brain which accepts as true the extravagant data of dreams." The only certain escape is death—at least, to the father of the narrator, who says: "You will understand that death is the only limitation imposed on human suffering." And in *The Dreamer,* the Vicomtesse speaks frequently of the omnipresence of death. Even as—or especially as—children, before we can understand the language of men, we sometimes stop in the midst of our games "to listen to the voice of death." And down through the years "it beckons to us." Death is always the available way out, which is why murder and suicide, provoked by fear, hatred, and despair, play such a role in Green's work.

Art and love are two partial means of escape. Art can be seen as catharsis: "If I did not put that madness into my books, who knows if it would not become installed in my life?" A poet "escapes from his self by transforming it."[12] Love, on the other hand, may serve to fill the emptiness of a life—love, in some cases, for anything or anybody, and over which one sometimes has no control. In *The Closed Garden* Adrienne says, "I did not choose you" to the doctor, and Eliane, in *The Strange River,* says about her secret love for her brother-in-law, "I did not choose him." A purely human love is involuntary and remains incomplete. It has value only when combined with divine love, in which the self is forgotten.

Green repeatedly stresses in his *Journal* that God offers the only liberation. "We do not know how to struggle against heaven, we do not know that one cannot win except by surrendering. There is no refuge from God except in God, says the Koran." Only the Church offers refuge outside time: "That is what explains in part the attraction that it exerts on many of us." And especially for those in despair or solitude, "Love and sometimes friendship outwit ordinary solitude, but supernatural solitude—only God can suppress it."[13] It follows that we should deliver ourselves to God and have confidence in Him, even if we do not understand: "God continually evades our miserable thoughts, and when we do address ourselves to Him, we never know the precise nature of our act, nor what effect it has on the invisible."[14] So one must strive to merit divine grace. That is the only escape.

Green's works have earned the respect and admiration of European readers. His plots are central to much human experience; his characters are powerfully drawn; his settings and atmosphere are most compelling in their uncanny blending of reality and hallucination; his penetration into the dark sources of human motivation are illuminating and convincing; and, to put it most simply, he knows how to tell a story. Why, then, has he failed to catch on in America? Perhaps one reason has already been suggested: it may be that Green's religious anguish with its body-soul, purity-impurity obsession is simply too alien to contemporary American experience, whereas Catholic France, seeing Green in a great tradition from Pascal through Baudelaire to Bernanos, finds his themes more familiar. Perhaps the American reader is disturbed by novels which begin on familiar solid ground and then proceed unexpectedly to dissolve into fantasy and the supernatural. We accept this in nineteenth-century Gothic fiction but perhaps not in a twentieth-century writer. Green has been criticized, as we have seen, on two other grounds: first, although he lived through two world wars, a depression, and any number of other social crises, there is no reflection whatsoever, no apparent awareness, of what is going on of crucial importance in the contemporary world; second, he is solely concerned with his personal vision—personal conflicts which he erects into universal problems. Some critics have admitted the power of his works but say that they are merely case studies of individual neuroses. Graham Greene implies something of this sort when he singles out for praise *The Strange River,* which he says shows "beautiful control"—the main character is "not left, like so many of Green's characters, nakedly exposed to life. Nor is he a clinical case. His cowardice is as universal as his patient licking of the wound."

But even Green's negative critics grant him an impressive talent, admitting that much of his power comes from his rendering his characters' thoughts and actions in terms of intense immediacy, of total involvement. He rarely indulges in the authorial prerogative of wandering outside the immediate context of his character's experience. Distinction between author and novel disappears, and this complete absorption is carried over to the reader. Green is the total artist. Insofar as it is possible to say this, he *lives,* he *is* his work. Once he begins a novel, he has no sense of where it is going. He begins it; he becomes totally engaged in it; and he lets it work out its own destiny. We may not always like what we find there; we may not accept all his problems as ours or agree with all his values; but of one thing we are certain: Green's novels are admirable blendings of art and life and, once experienced, are unforgettable. They are powerful documentations of the sense of alienation and loss that haunts modern man and of the devastating consequences when man can no longer harmonize his physical life with the invisible spiritual world that lies beyond.

Notes and References

Chapter One

1. In his later writings Green gives an interesting picture of his early problems with language as a result of being raised bilingually. His first language was French, which he spoke at school and at home, whenever possible. As a small boy, he says, English did not sound like a real language to him. His mother had mixed feelings about this, but she was often amazed, and called Julian her "little Frenchman." Even as a young man, when at the University of Virginia, he was diffident and most uncertain about his English—though it was not long before he spoke and wrote it like a native American. But he found it difficult to concentrate on learning one "foreign" language when he was a student of so many. While he read the King James Bible closely, he also studied his native French, read the Vulgate Latin Scriptures, and knew German well. He also took up the study of Hebrew in order to have access to the original Scriptures and to try to resolve problems raised by contradictory translations. This multilingual talent had some curious effects. For example, he notes that when writing in English his work took a different form than when writing in French. He tended to say "different things." He explains this by noting that the French language tends toward the abstract, whereas English has a "more primitive element" preserved from earlier times, an element almost totally lacking in French. For him, Latinized words have an "intellectual beauty," whereas Anglo-Saxon has a "barbaric beauty." French could never give an emotionally disturbing word such as "doom"— it would say "final judgment," with a direct appeal to the intellect. " 'Jugement dernier' makes one think, but 'crack of doom' makes you run for cover." "An Experiment in English," *Harper's*, 183 (September, 1941), 397-405, and "Translation and the 'Fields of Scripture,' " *American Scholar*, 11 (January, 1942), 110-21.

2. See I. W. Brock, "Julien Green: A Biographical and Literary Sketch," *French Review*, 23 (March, 1950), 347-59. I differ with Brock in certain matters of fact and interpretation, but I am also indebted to his article in my brief account of Green's career.

3. *Journal*, III, 83-84.

4. Published in the *University of Virginia Magazine*, 63 (Session 1919-20).

5. Fillmore Norfleet in a letter, May 12, 1945, as cited by Brock.

6. Brock, 352.

7. Interview with Green, September 16, 1968.

8. *Memories of Happy Days*, p. 265. Cited by Brock.

9. Cahiers de Paris, 1927. Two of these essays appeared in English: "Charlotte Brontë and Her Sisters," *Virginia Quarterly Review*, 5 (January, 1929); and "William Blake, Prophet," *Virginia Quarterly Review*, 5 (April, 1929). Also attesting to Green's interest in Anglo-American literature was his *Un Puritain homme de lettres: Nathaniel Hawthorne* (Paris, 1928).

10. Green himself rejects the term; he disapproves of all "labels." Interview, September 10, 1968.

11. Brian Fitch, *Configuration critique de Julien Green* (Paris, 1966), p. 15.

12. Green, *To Leave Before Dawn*, p. 24. (Hereafter referred to as *To Leave*.)

13. *To Leave*, pp. 10-11.

14. *To Leave*, pp. 31-32.

15. *To Leave*, p. 33.

16. *To Leave*, pp. 64-65.

17. *To Leave*, p. 58.

18. *To Leave*, p. 8.

19. Robert de Saint Jean, *Julien Green par lui-même*, p. 131.

20. Janine Carrel, *L'Expérience du seuil dans L'oeuvre de Julien Green*, p. 13.

21. Saint Jean, p. 163.

22. Interview with Green, September 16, 1968.

23. *Oeuvres complètes*, III, 102.

24. Green, *Vers l'invisible*. Cited by Saint Jean, p. 167.

25. Saint Jean, pp. 129-30.

26. Steps and stairways recur frequently in Green's writings, both because they loomed large in Green's own boyhood and because he seemed, as a writer, to unconsciously endow them with a special significance. Mircea Eliade has commented on the symbolic meaning of ladder and stair imagery in general and specifically in the works of Green. Such imagery, says Eliade, "gives plastic expression to the break through the planes necessitated by the passage from one mode of being to another, by placing us at the cosmological point where communication between Heaven, Earth, and Hell becomes possible." Symbolism of stair climbing belongs to the archaic content of the human psyche, and Julian Green, according to Eliade, gives an example of "a spontaneous rediscovery of this primordial symbolism." He quotes Green's *Journal* of April 4, 1933, where Green says: "In all my books, the idea of fear or of any other fairly strong emotion

seems linked in some inexplicable manner to a staircase. I realised this yesterday, whilst I was passing in review all the novels I have written. . . . I wonder how I can have so often repeated this effect without noticing it. As a child, I used to dream I was being chased on a staircase. My mother had the same fears in her younger days; perhaps something of them has remained with me." Eliade goes on to say that "we now know why the idea of fear, for Julian Green, was associated with the image of a staircase, and why all the dramatic events he described in his works—love, death, or crime— happened upon a staircase. The act of climbing or ascending symbolises *the way towards absolute reality;* and to the profane consciousness, the approach toward that reality arouses an ambivalent feeling, of fear and of joy, of attraction and repulsion, etc. The ideas of sanctification, of death, love, and deliverance are all involved in the symbolism of stairs. Indeed, each of these modes of being represents a cessation of the profane human condition; that is, a breaking of the ontological plane. Through love and death, sanctity and metaphysical knowledge, man passes . . . from the 'unreal to the reality.' " The stairway, therefore, is a "center" between different levels of being and makes communication between them possible. *Images and Symbols; Studies in Religious Symbolism* (New York, 1961), pp. 50-51.

27. Interview with Green, September 10, 1968.

Chapter Two

1. JV, pp. 266, 1103.

2. Written in 1924 and included in the volume entitled *Voyageur sur la Terre* (Paris, 1927) and in *Christine and Other Stories* (New York, 1930).

3. First published in the *Nouvelle Revue Française,* August and September, 1926.

4. Published in the *University of Virginia Magazine,* 63 (Session 1919-20), 334-46.

5. "How I Wrote My First Novel," *French Books Month by Month* (May-June 1927), pp. 71-73.

6. Saint Jean, p. 71.

7. Saint Jean, p. 71.

8. Published in *Revue de Paris,* December 1, 1927; and appeared as a book the following year.

9. JV, p. 3161.

10. Saint Jean, p. 74.

Chapter Three

1. Translated by Marshall A. Best (New York, 1927).

2. Julian Green has commented in *To Leave Before Dawn* that

his concern for fire was fixed during his boyhood—especially during
a long cold winter in wartime France, when life did indeed seem
to revolve around the possession of a few pieces of coal.

3. Translated by Henry Longan Stuart (New York, 1928).

4. Translated by Vyvyan Holland (New York, 1929).

5. Translated by Vyvyan Holland (New York, 1932).

6. Robert de Saint Jean, p. 67. Writing in his *Journal* of June 13,
1941, Green expressed his view that *Épaves* was "my best novel,
my most *grown up* [these two words in English] book, the most
difficult to write, the most thoughtful, the most difficult to read also."

7. Saint Jean, p. 68.

8. Janine Carrel, *L'Expérience du seuil dans l'oeuvre de Julien
Green* (Zurich, 1967), pp. 27-28.

9. Green says that in this "foolish self-worship" "*I loved myself
pure* [his italics]. . . . I never looked at myself naked, nakedness
being impure, and finally believed, in a vague way, that my entire
person was one of those only to be seen dressed and never to be
touched, under any circumstances. My mother was the only one
who could kiss me." *To Leave,* pp. 149-50.

10. *To Leave,* p. 74.

11. As recounted in Robert Graves, *The Greek Myths,* I (Penguin
edition, 1955), 286-88.

Chapter Four

1. *Saturday Review,* 14 (September 5, 1936), 7.

2. Saint Jean, p. 87.

3. Saint Jean, p. 77.

4. Translated by Vyvyan Holland (New York, 1934).

5. "Comment j'ai écrit *Le Visionnaire,*" *Annuel Politique et Littéraire,* 101 (November 3, 1933), 505-6.

6. "Comment j'ai écrit *Le Visionnaire,*" 505-6.

7. Translated by Vyvyan Holland (New York, 1936).

8. *L'Europe nouvelle,* 19 (May 23, 1936), 550-51.

9. Marcel, 550-51.

10. Translated by James Witall (New York, 1941).

11. The god Varouna (Varuna) has been described variously: as
the administrator of cosmic law, as one who regulates all activities
in this world, as the lord of human morality who ensures that no
transgression against the law, cosmic or human, will go unpunished.
Mircea Eliade defines the symbolism of Varuna as follows: he is the
"god who binds"; therefore his worshipers have many religious
ceremonies devoted to releasing man from the "toils of Varuna,"
even though they recognize that the god usually imprisons only the
wicked. Varuna is also god of the sky and, at times, the sea, with

the stars as "eyes": he *sees* all, *knows* all, and can *do* anything. He punishes the wicked by bondage"; that is, he inflicts illness or impotence on anyone who infringes on the universal order. He is primarily nocturnal; he "envelops like the darkness" and surrounds everything. The god of night is himself "virtuality," seed, the non-manifest, which enables him to become the god of waters and to envelop Vritra, the "demon." But Varuna sometimes tends, in binding, to arrest life, even to bring death. Eliade, *Images and Symbols; Studies in Religious Symbolism,* trans. Philip Moiret (New York, 1961), p. 92.

12. JV, p. 180.
13. Saint Jean, p. 88.
14. Saint Jean, p. 89.
15. Translated by J. H. F. McEwen (New York, 1949).
16. Saint Jean, p. 91.
17. Saint Jean, p. 93, referring to JV, p. 591.
18. *Journal,* II, 143-44.
19. *To Leave,* p. 52.
20. JV, p. 478.
21. JV, p. 596.

Chapter Five

1. *Terre Lointaine,* p. 33.
2. *Terre Lointaine,* p. 53.
3. *Terre Lointaine,* pp. 53-54.
4. *Terre Lointaine,* pp. 102-3.
5. The source of the title appears to be one of Pascal's *Pensées:* "Who knows if that other half of life when we think we are awake is not another sleep only slightly different from the first, from which we awake when we believe ourselves asleep?"
6. Translated by Anne Green (New York, 1957).
7. Introduction to *Le Malfaiteur,* in *Oeuvres complètes* (Paris, 1955), p. 244.
8. Introduction to *Le Malfaiteur,* p. 245.
9. Saint Jean, pp. 99-100.
10. Saint Jean, p. 100.
11. *New Yorker,* 29 (April 18, 1953), 115-16.
12. Marilyn Gaddis Rose, "Julian Green, Novelist as Playwright," *Modern Drama,* Vol. 6, No. 2 (September, 1963), pp. 195-203.
13. When asked what he meant by the statement that other writers had spoiled a "great and noble subject," Green replied: "Homosexuality is, for the Christian, only one aspect of the much larger problem of sexuality.... If I had given *Sud* another title, 'The Lieutenant Ian,' for example, the parallel with *Moira* might have

been more easily grasped, and more instructive. For Joseph Day as for Wiczewski, in fact, an imperative sexuality is accompanied by a hatred for the sexual instinct, for these two men are at once carnal and spiritual, and perhaps drawn more by the high than by the low." Quoted by Saint Jean, p. 105.

14. It has been suggested that the dates of events in the play were not chosen by chance. The action takes place on April 11 and 12, 1861, and at the precise moment that the play ends—at 4:20 A.M. on April 12—the first shot of the Civil War was fired on Fort Sumter. J. C. Trewin, *Plays of the Year* (London, 1955), p. 11.

15. See pp. 33, 53-54.

16. Rose, 196.

17. It should be pointed out that one member of the audience had high praise for *Sud,* which he put in the form of a letter to Green. Albert Camus' interesting letter is reproduced in Saint Jean, p. 107.

18. Epigraph to *Julien Green par lui-même.*

Chapter Six

1. Translated by Denise Folliot (New York, 1951).

2. R. E. Batchelor, "L'Art de l'allusion dans *Moira,*" *Nottingham French Studies,* 5 (1966), 40-49.

3. *To Leave,* p. 145.

4. Published 1960, translated by Anne Green (New York, 1961).

5. Saint Jean, p. 126.

6. Saint Jean, p. 119.

7. Saint Jean, p. 127.

8. *Journal,* III, 50; II, 11.

9. *Journal,* VI, 208, 248.

10. *Journal,* VI, 297.

11. *Journal, III,* 75.

12. *Journal,* I, 136; III, 13.

13. *Journal,* III, 13, 40; IV, 28.

14. *Journal,* IV, 28.

Selected Bibliography

All works listed were published in Paris unless
otherwise indicated.

Bibliographies

HOY, PETER C. *Essai de bibliographie des études en langue française
consacrée à Julien Green (1923-1967).* Paris: Lettres modernes,
1970. 320 pp.
————. *Exposition Julien Green, 1900- .* Catalog of manuscripts,
original editions, translations, photographs, documents. Maison
française d'Oxford, 1970. (N.p.)
ROSE, MARILYN GADDIS. "Julian Green and Anglo-American Critics,
a Selected Bibliography," *Bulletin of Bibliography.* May-August,
1963. pp. 17-19.

PRIMARY WORKS

Books and Stories by Julian Green

"The Apprentice Psychiatrist," *University of Virginia Magazine,*
LXIII (Session 1919-20), 334-46.
Pamphlet contre les catholiques de France, La Revue de Pamphlétaires,
No. 1 (October 15, 1924), under pseudonym of Théophile
Delaporte. Reprinted as book, with foreword by the author
and preface by Jacques Maritain. Paris: Plon, 1963. 83 pp.
Mont-Cinère (novel). Plon, Coll. "L'Aubier," 1926. (*Avarice House.*
Trans. Marshall A. Best. New York, 1927.)
Adrienne Mesurat (novel). Plon, Coll. "Le Roseau d'Or," 1927. (*The
Closed Garden.* Trans. Henry Longan Stuart. New York, 1928.)
Christine (story). Abbeville, Coll. "Les Amis d'Edouard," No. 120,
1927.
Suite anglaise (collection of critical essays). Les Cahiers de Paris,
1927.
Le Voyageur sur la Terre (story). Editions de la Nouvelle Revue
Française, Coll. "Une Oeuvre, un Portrait," 1927.
Les Clefs de la mort (story). Editions de la Pléiade, 1928.
Un Puritain homme de lettres: Nathaniel Hawthorne. Toulouse, Aux
Editions des Cahiers Libres, 1928.

149

"Léviathan (story) in *Christine suivi de Léviathan.* Toulouse, Aux Editions des Cahiers Libres, Coll. "Losanges," No. 2, 1928.

Léviathan (novel). Plon, Coll. "Le Roseau d'Or," 1929. (*The Dark Journey.* Trans. Vyvyan Holland. New York, 1929.)

Le Voyageur sur la Terre, collection including "Christine" (1924), "Les Clefs de la Mort" (1927), "Léviathan" (1927), and "Le Voyageur sur la Terre" (1926). Paris, 1930. (*Christine and Other Stories.* Trans. Courtney Bruerton. New York, 1930.)

L'Autre Sommeil (novel). Nouvelle Revue Française, 1931.

Épaves (novel). Plon, Coll. "La Palatine," 1932. (*The Strange River.* Trans. Vyvyan Holland. New York, 1932.)

Le Visionnaire (novel). Plon, Coll. "La Palatine," 1932. (*The Dreamer.* Trans. Vyvyan Holland. New York, 1932.)

Minuit (novel). Plon, Coll. "La Palatine," 1936. (*Midnight.* Trans. Vyvyan Holland. New York, 1936.)

Journal, I (1928-1934). Plon, Coll. "La Palatine," 1938.

Journal, II (1935-1939). Plon, Coll. "La Palatine," 1939.

Personal Record (1928-1939) Trans. Jocelyn Godefroi. New York: Harper, 1939. 342 pp.

Varouna (novel). Plon, Coll. "La Palatine," 1940. (*Then Shall the Dust Return.* Trans. James Witall. New York, 1941.)

Journal, III (1940-1943). Plon, Coll. "L'Épi," 1946.

Memories of Happy Days. New York: Harper, 1942.

Si j'étais vous . . . (novel). Plon, Coll. "Originales," 1947. (*If I Were You.* Trans. J. H. P. McEwen. New York, 1949.

Journal, IV (1943-1945). Plon, Coll. "L'Épi," 1949.

Moira (novel). Plon, Coll. "L'Épi," 1950. (*Moira.* Trans. Denise Folliot. New York, 1951.)

Journal, V (1946-1950). Plon, Coll. "L'Épi," 1951.

Journal, VI (1950-1954). Plon, Coll. "L'Épi," 1955.

Le Malfaiteur (novel) in *Oeuvres complètes,* "Romans IV (1936-1937)." Plon, 1955. (*The Transgressor.* Trans. Anne Green. New York, 1957.)

Le Bel Aujourd'hui (Journal VII, 1955-58). Plon, 1958.

Chaque homme dans sa nuit (novel). Plon, 1960. (*Each in His Darkness.* Trans. Anne Green. New York, 1961.)

Journal (1928-1958). Plon, 1961. (One-volume edition.)

Partir avant le jour (Autobiographie I). Grasset, Coll. "Cahiers Verts," 1963. (*To Leave Before Dawn.* Trans. Anne Green, New York, 1967.)

Mille chemins ouverts (Autobiographie II). Grasset, Coll. "Cahiers Verts," 1964.

Diary, 1928-1957. Selected by Kurt Wolff. Trans. Anne Green. New York: Harcourt Brace, 1964.

Terre lointaine (Autobiographie III). Grasset, Coll. "Cahiers Verts," 1966.

Vers l'invisible [*Journal VIII* (1958-1967).] Plon, 1967.

Journal. Tome I: 1928-1949; Tome II: 1949-1966. Plon, 1969. Edition in two volumes.

Les Années faciles. (Journal 1926-1934.) Plon, 1970. New and definitive edition.

Si j'étais vous . . . (novel). Plon, 1970. New and definitive edition.

L'Autre (novel). Plon, 1971.

Articles by Julian Green

"Dedalus par James Joyce," *Nouvelle Revue Française*, XXIII (July-December, 1924), 246-49.

"Samuel Johnson," *Revue hebdomadaire*, January 3, 1925. (Reprinted in *Suite Anglaise*. Paris: Les Cahiers de Paris, 1927.)

"Portrait d'un grand conteur américain, Nathaniel Hawthorne," *Les Nouvelles Littéraires*, January 15, 1927.

"How I Wrote My First Novel," *French Books Month by Month* (May-June, 1927), pp. 71-73.

"La Vie Mélancolique de Charles Lamb," *Revue Universelle*, October 15, 1927. (Reprinted in *Suite Anglaise*. Paris, 1927.)

"Charlotte Brontë and Her Sisters," *Virginia Quarterly Review*, V (January, 1929), 42-58.

"William Blake, Prophet," *Virginia Quarterly Review*, V (April, 1929), 220-32. (Originally published as "William Blake, prophète," *Revue Européenne*, October, 1926. Reprinted in *Suite Anglaise*. Paris, 1927.)

"Comment j'ai écrit *Le Visionnaire*," *Annales Politiques et Littéraires*, CI, No. 3, or November 3, 1933, 505-6.

"Experiment in English," *Harper's Magazine*, 183 (September, 1941), 397-405.

"How a Novelist Begins," *Atlantic*, 168 (December, 1941), 749-52.

"Translation and the Fields of Scripture," *American Scholar*, XI (January, 1942), 110-21.

"Souvenirs (Quand nous habitons tous ensemble)," *Les Oeuvres nouvelles*, II. New York: Editions de la Maison française, Inc., 1943. Pp. 9-45.

"Passy," *Commonweal*, XXXVIII (June 4, 1943), 162-63.

"A Steamer Letter," *Commonweal*, XLIII (January 4, 1946), 301.

"Souvenir de Poe," *Figaro littéraire*, No. 13 (1946).

Translations by Green

(With Anne Green). *Basic Verities of Charles Péguy*. New York: Pantheon Books, 1943.

(With Anne Green). *Men and Saints by Charles Péguy*. New York, 1944.

The Mystery of the Charity of Joan of Arc (Charles Péguy). New York, 1950.

Plays by Green

Sud. Paris: Plon, 1953.
L'Ennemi. Paris: Plon, 1954.
L'Ombre. Paris: Plon, 1956.

SECONDARY WORKS

*A Selected Bibliography of Works Concerned
Primarily with Julian Green*

BRISVILLE, JEAN CLAUDE. *À la rencontre de Julien Green*. Paris: Editions La Sixaine, 1947. 44 pp. A brief survey of Green's life and works and "Green's universe." (See also Brisville's *Julien Green*. Gand, 1947. 44 pp.)

BRODIN, PIERRE. *Julien Green*. Paris: Editions Universitaires, 1957. 128 pp. A brief but useful survey of Green's writings. Includes a chronology; "aspects of biography"; a chapter on "influences," which is largely a recitation of names; and chapters on themes, characterization, and technique. Gives excerpts from the journals. A good introduction offering perceptive if necessarily undeveloped comments on Green's work.

CARREL, JANINE. *L'expérience du seuil dans l'oeuvre de Julien Green*. Zurich: Juris Druck, 1967. 112 pp. Brief but intensive study of the "two realities" of Green's world—the sense of imprisonment and need to escape. Generous quotations from Green's texts and an explicative commentary. Short bibliography.

COOKE, MOTHER M. GERARD. "Hallucination and Death as Motifs of Escape in the Novels of Julien Green." Dissertation published in *Studies in Romance Languages and Literatures*, LXII (1960). The Catholic University of America. A useful study of psychological motifs in Green's work, in the light of Freud, Stekel, and other psychologists.

EIGELDINGER, MARC. *Julien Green et la tentation de l'irréel*. Paris: Editions des Portes de France, 1947. 101 pp. Good study of one of the most important aspects of Green's work, but published too early to include some of Green's major later writings.

FITCH, BRIAN T. (ed.). *Configuration critique de Julien Green*. Paris: Lettres Modernes, 1966. 189 pp. Contains five studies of different aspects of Green's works by several authors: two by Fitch, one each by Peter C. Hoy, Cedric R. P. May, and Annette Lavers. Perceptive and erudite examinations of such elements as dream imagery, personality, time, space, and immobility in Green's writings.

FONGARO, ANTOINE. *L'Existence dans les Romans de Julien Green.* Rome: Angelo Signorelli, 1954. 185 pp. A useful study of Green's major themes: destiny, solitude, time, suffering, and attempts to escape. Brief bibliography. No index.

GORKINE, MICHEL. *Julien Green.* Paris: Nouvelles Editions Debresse, 1956. 218 pp. A good introduction and survey of Green's works. A standard study available in many libraries.

JOYE, JEAN-CLAUDE. *Julian Green et le monde de la fatalité.* Berne: Armand Druck, 1964. 252 pp. Doctoral dissertation.

MUFF, OSWALD. *La Dialectique du Néant et du Désir dans l'oeuvre de Julien Green.* Zurich: Imprimerie P. G. Keller, 1967. 127 pp.

PETIT, JACQUES. *Julien Green, "L'homme qui venait d'ailleurs."* Paris: Desclée de Brouwer, 1969. 349 pp. A major study devoted to Green's search for the self, the conviction that the self alone is the subject of his works. Examines stages in Green's quest for the truth about himself and the means of telling it accurately. A comprehensive and detailed analysis, drawn entirely from primary sources. No bibliography.

PRÉVOST, JEAN-LAURENT. *Julien Green, ou L'âme engagée.* Lyon: Editions Emmanuel Vitte, 1960. 160 pp. Part I deals with relations between Green and André Gide. Part II discusses Green as two men, one related to the soul, the other to the body. Also examines the influence of childhood on Green's writing and compares his work with that of Mauriac, Dostoevsky, Baudelaire, and Gide. Interesting.

ROUSSEAU, GUY NOËL. *Sur le chemin de Julien Green. Un essai et des documents.* Neuchâtel; a la Baconnière, 1967. 53 pp. Brief but useful introduction with illustrative excerpts from Green's writings.

SAINT JEAN, ROBERT DE. *Julien Green par Lui-même.* Paris: Aux Editions de Seuil, 1967. 188 pp. An excellent short introduction to Green's life and work by a friend of many years. Includes brief but well-chosen samples of Green's writings, comments by Green himself available nowhere else, and succinct critical observations by Saint Jean. Photographs, chronology, and bibliography.

SEMOLUÉ, JEAN. *Julien Green ou l'obsession du mal.* Paris: Editions du Centurion, 1964. 190 pp. An important study of a central aspect of Green's work, covering most of his major writings.

STOKES, SAMUEL. *Julian Green and the Thorn of Puritanism.* New York: Columbia University Press, 1955. 151 pp. Originally a doctoral dissertation, this study confines itself to exploring the spiritual backgrounds of Green's novels. It examines Green's Christian heritage, his obsession with death, the influence of Puritanism and Buddhism. A good presentation of important elements in Green's thought and experience.

Articles about Julian Green

ALBRECHT, MILTON C. "A Study of Julian Green," *Journal of Abnormal and Social Psychology*, XLI (April, 1946), 169-88.

————. "Psychological Motives in the Fiction of Julian Green," *Journal of Personality*, XVI (March 16, 1948), 278-303.

BECK, THEODORE TOULON. "Julian Green: His Southern Background," *Georgia Review*, VII (Spring, 1953), 89-98.

BERNIER, FERNAND. "Le Sentiment religieux chez Julien Green," *Revue de l'Université Laval*, Vol. XVII, Nos. 5 and 6 (January-February, 1963), pp. 420-44, 520-38, 611-33, 716-30.

BESPALOV, RACHEL. "Julien Green," *Nouvelle Revue Française*, XLVI (March 1, 1936), 416-27.

BRACE, MARJORIE. "The Case of Julian Green," *Accent*, II (Autumn, 1941), 42-44.

CABANIS, JOSÉ. "Julien Green et le Royaume de Dieu," *Table Ronde*, No. 172 (1962), 53-59.

CLUNY, CLAUDE MICHEL. "Eros et Virginie," *Nouvelle Revue Française*, XIV (July, 1966), 107-11.

DARBELNET, J. L. "Un écrivain américain d'expression française: Julien Green," *Bulletin des Études française*, No. 25 (May-June, 1945), 3-15.

FRANK, JOSEPH. "Notes on the Literary Situation," *Partisan Review*, XVIII (July, 1951), 452.

GRUSON-KARPLUS, ANNE. "Esthétique de l'imaginaire dans les romans de Julian Green," *French Review*, Vol. XXXV, No. 6 (May, 1962), pp. 539-45.

KEATING, L. CLARK. "Julian Green and Nathaniel Hawthorne," *French Review*, XXVIII (May, 1955), pp. 485-92.

LEHNER, FREDERICK. "Julian Green," *French Review*, XV (February, 1942), pp. 385-94.

PICON, GAËTAN. "Julien Green et Varouna," *Cahiers du Sud*, No. 239 October, 1941), pp. 500-10.

————. "Sur Julien Green," *Fontaine*, No. 55 (October, 1946), pp. 443-51.

POULET, GEORGES. "L'univers double de Julien Green," *Preuves*, No. 200 (October, 1967), pp. 18-33.

PRÉVOST, JEAN-LAURENT. "Julien Green: le drame spirituel," *Table Ronde*, Nos. 103-4 (July-August, 1956), pp. 220-29.

Rose, Marilyn Gaddis. "Julian Green: Bilingual Novelist," *ETC*, XXI (June, 1964), pp. 165-73.

————. "Julian Green's Heroine, the American Child-Woman: To Escape through Delusion and Death," *Forum* (Houston), III (Fall, 1961), pp. 29-33.

Sénart, Philippe. "Julian Green," *Table Ronde*, No. 214 (1965), pp. 50-58.

Talon, Henri A. "Julian Green: The American-born French Novelist,' *Yale French Studies*, No. 10 (1952-53), pp. 29-42.

Viatte, Auguste. "Julien Green devant l'impureté," *Revue de l'Université Laval*, VI (March, 1951), pp. 598-602.

Books Which Include Chapters or Sections on Julian Green

Albérès, R. M. *Les hommes traqués*. Paris: La Nouvelle Edition, 1953. Pp. 113-54.

Arland, Marcel. *Essais et nouveaux essais critiques*. Paris: Gallimard, 1952. Pp. 248-51.

Borne, Alain. *Problèmes du roman*. Lyon: Confluences, 1943.

Brée, Germaine, and Margaret Guiton. *An Age of Fiction: The French Novel from Gide to Camus*. New York: Rutgers, 1957. Revised edition, under title of *The French Novel from Gide to Camus*. New York: Harcourt, Brace & World, 1962. Also in paperback. Harbinger edition, pp. 101-5.

Brodin, Pierre. *Les Ecrivains français de l'entre-guerre*. Montreal, 1943. Pp. 297-312. New edition. New York: Brentano's, 1945. Pp. 269-84.

Jaloux, Edmond. *D'Eschyle à Giraudoux*. Fribourg: Egloff, 1946. Pp. 273-78.

Moeller, Charles. *Littérature du XXᵉ Siècle et Christianisme*. Vol. I: *Silence de Dieu*. Paris: Casterman, 1953. Pp. 302-70.

Peyre, Henri. *French Novelists of Today*. Oxford University Press, 1967. Galaxy paperback edition. Pp. 195-208.

Picon, Gaëtan. *Panorama de la Nouvelle littérature française*. Introductions, illustrations, documents. Paris: Editions du Point du Jour, 1949. Pp. 96-99. New edition. Gallimard, 1960.

Rousseaux, André. *Littérature au Vingtième Siècle*, Vol. II. Paris: Albin Michel, 1939. Pp. 87-95. New edition, 1948, pp. 77-93.

Thérive, André. *Galerie de ce temps*. Paris: La Nouvelle Revue critique, 1931. Pp. 129-41.

Index

(The works of Julian Green are listed under his name)

157